Family Circle®
HOMETOWN COOKING®

D0904624

Volume 9
Meredith® Consumer Marketing
Des Moines, Iowa

Family Circle. Hometown Cooking.

Meredith. Consumer Marketing
Consumer Marketing Product Director: Heather Sorensen
Consumer Marketing Product Manager: Wendy Merical
Consumer Marketing Billing/Renewal Manager: Tami Beachem
Business Director: Ron Clingman
Senior Production Manager: Al Rodruck

Waterbury Publications, Inc.
Editorial Director: Lisa Kingsley
Associate Editor: Tricia Bergman
Associate Editor/Food Stylist: Annie Peterson
Assistant Food Stylist: Skyler Myers
Creative Director: Ken Carlson
Associate Design Director: Doug Samuelson
Production Assistant: Mindy Samuelson
Indexer: Mary Williams
Contributing Food Stylist: Charlie Worthington
Contributing Copy Editors: Terri Fredrickson, Peg Smith

Family Circle. **Magazine**
Editor in Chief: Linda Fears
Design Director: Lisa Kelsey
Food Director: Regina Ragone, M.S., R.D.
Executive Food Editor: Julie Miltenberger
Associate Food Editor: Michael Tyrrell
Associate Food Editor: Melissa Knific

Meredith National Media Group
President: Tom Harty

Meredith Corporation
Chairman and Chief Executive Officer: Stephen M. Lacy

In Memoriam: E.T. Meredith III (1933–2003)

Pictured on the front cover:
Key Lime Coconut Cake with Marshmallow Frosting
(recipe on page 169)
Photography by Jason Donnelly

Enjoy prizewinning recipes from hometown America!

The best recipes are those that have been created, tried, tested, and perfected by dedicated cooks who truly love the process of coming up with something wonderful to feed to family and friends—and that may win first place in a recipe contest or earn a blue ribbon at the state fair. Striving for innovation and perfection keeps competitive cooks working away in the kitchen, trying a pinch of this and a little bit of that. They make dishes again and again—asking family, friends, and coworkers to be judges and taste-testers—until they get the result they're looking for. *Family Circle Hometown Cooking* is packed with those kinds of recipes. Every page features the very best recipes from America's hometown cooks.

As you peruse the pages of this book, you'll meet some of the cooks who contributed recipes and hear their heartwarming stories. When you cook from it, you'll taste why they are winners.

— **The Editors**

table of contents

CHAPTER 1
getting started

A selection of these savory nibbles can start the party—or be the party!

SAVORY ROSEMARY, PANCETTA,
AND FIG CHEESECAKE

COLD APPETIZERS

Avocado-Deviled Eggs, 22

Cheese Wafers with Pepper Jelly, 23

Savory Rosemary, Pancetta, and Fig Cheesecake, 19

DIPS AND SPREADS

Cheesy Skillet Artichoke Dip, 20

Cucumber-Feta Dip, 21

Sweet Potato Wedges with Hummus, 16

HOT APPETIZERS

Cheddar-Beer Weenies, 16

Cornmeal Griddle Cakes with Sautéed Corn, 14

Cuban Drummies, 11

Cubanitos, 13

Grilled Vegetable Platter, 15

Oven-Baked Sicilian Meatballs, 8

Stuffed Sausage Sliders, 12

NUTS AND SNACKS

Chile Pecans, 24

Cinnamon Pretzels, 25

Oven-Baked Sicilian Meatballs

Sicilians favor sweet-savory flavors. In these tasty meatballs Parmesan cheese, herbs, and Italian sausage provide the savory, while dried currants provide the sweet.

MAKES 24 servings **PREP** 25 minutes **BAKE** 25 minutes

⅔   **cup soft bread crumbs**
3   **tablespoons milk**
1   **egg, lightly beaten**
⅓   **cup grated Parmesan cheese**
¼   **cup finely chopped onion**
¼   **cup snipped fresh basil**
3   **tablespoons pine nuts, toasted***
3   **tablespoons dried currants**
½   **teaspoon salt**
1   **clove garlic, minced**
¼   **teaspoon freshly ground black pepper**
1   **pound bulk sweet Italian sausage**
    Pasta sauce, warmed (optional)

1 Preheat oven to 350°F. In a large bowl combine bread crumbs and milk. Let stand 5 minutes. Stir in egg, Parmesan cheese, onion, basil, pine nuts, currants, salt, garlic, and black pepper. Add sausage; mix well.

2 Shape mixture into 24 meatballs. Place in a single layer on a 15×10×1-inch baking pan. Bake, uncovered, 25 to 30 minutes or until meatballs are done (160°F). Drain off fat. If desired, serve with pasta sauce for dipping.

*Toast small amounts of nuts or finely chopped nuts, coconut, or seeds in a dry skillet over medium heat for 2 minutes or until fragrant and golden, stirring frequently.

PER SERVING 58 **CAL**; 3 g **FAT** (1 g **SAT**); 16 mg **CHOL**; 199 mg **SODIUM**; 3 g **CARB**; 0 g **FIBER**; 4 g **PRO**

Cuban Drummies

In Cuba and other parts of the Caribbean, a spicy-sweet sauce called mojo [MOH-hoh] livens up roasted and grilled meats, poultry, and fish. The marinade for these drummies—made with citrus juice, herbs, vinegar, jalapeño, and mango nectar—is essentially a mojo. Some of the marinade is reserved and blended with fresh mango, onion, and cilantro to make a dipping sauce.

MAKES 12 servings **PREP** 20 minutes **MARINATE** 2 hours **BAKE** 25 minutes

12	**chicken wings (about 2 pounds)***
1	**cup mango nectar**
½	**cup lemon juice**
½	**cup orange juice**
½	**cup snipped fresh Italian parsley**
¼	**cup red wine vinegar**
¼	**cup olive oil**
1	**to 2 fresh jalapeños**, seeded and finely chopped**
6	**cloves garlic, minced**
1	**teaspoon salt**
½	**teaspoon ground cumin**
1	**mango, seeded, peeled, and chopped**
⅓	**cup chopped onion**
¼	**cup snipped fresh cilantro**
	Orange wedges and/or fresh cilantro (optional)

1 Cut off and discard tips of chicken wings or reserve for making broth. Cut wings at joints to make 24 pieces. Place chicken in a resealable plastic bag set in a shallow dish.

2 For marinade, in a medium bowl whisk together mango nectar, lemon juice, orange juice, parsley, vinegar, oil, jalapeño pepper, garlic, salt, and cumin. Remove ½ cup of the marinade for sauce; cover and chill until needed.

3 Pour the remaining marinade over chicken. Seal bag; turn to coat chicken. Marinate in the refrigerator 2 to 24 hours, turning bag occasionally.

4 Preheat oven to 450°F. Drain chicken, discarding marinade. Arrange chicken in a single layer on the unheated rack of a large broiler pan. Bake 25 minutes or until chicken is golden brown, turning once.

5 Meanwhile, for sauce, in a blender combine the reserved ½ cup marinade, the mango, onion, and cilantro. Cover and blend until smooth. Serve chicken with sauce and, if desired, orange wedges and/or fresh cilantro.

***Tip** Or use 24 chicken wing drumettes and continue in Step 1 with placing chicken in a resealable plastic bag.

****Tip** Chile peppers contain oils that can irritate skin and eyes. Wear plastic or rubber gloves when working with them.

PER SERVING 278 **CAL**; 20 g **FAT** (4 g **SAT**); 97 mg **CHOL**; 283 mg **SODIUM**; 9 g **CARB**; 1 g **FIBER**; 17 g **PRO**

Stuffed Sausage Sliders

These pork sausage patties infused with apple, garlic, fennel, and herbs feature flavors perfect for a fall party. Better yet, they're topped with a Grilled Apple-Fennel Slaw flavored with vinegar, brown sugar, butter, and a spike of cayenne.

MAKES 16 servings **PREP** 40 minutes **CHILL** 1 hour **GRILL** 10 minutes

1   **small apple**
2   **tablespoons olive oil**
3   **cloves garlic, minced**
1½   **teaspoons cracked black pepper**
1   **teaspoon fennel seeds, crushed**
¾   **teaspoon salt**
¼   **to ½ teaspoon dried thyme or sage, crushed**
⅛   **teaspoon grated whole nutmeg**
2   **pounds ground pork**
½   **to ¾ cup shredded white cheddar cheese or smoked provolone cheese (2 to 3 ounces)**
16   **2-inch buns sliced nearly in half**
1   **recipe Grilled Apple-Fennel Slaw**

1 Peel and shred enough of the apple to measure ⅓ cup; place in a large bowl. Add oil, garlic, pepper, fennel seeds, salt, thyme, and nutmeg. Add ground pork; mix well.

2 For each patty, shape a scant ¼ cup pork mixture into a ball and use your finger to make a deep indentation in top. Fill indentation with 1 to 2 teaspoons cheese. Reshape pork mixture to enclose filling. Shape into a ball and flatten into a 2½-inch-diameter patty. Place on a baking sheet. Cover and chill for 1 hour or up to 4 hours.

3 Grill patties, covered, over medium heat 10 to 12 minutes or until done (160°F), turning once.

4 Serve patties in buns topped with Grilled Apple-Fennel Slaw. Secure with a pick, if desired.

Grilled Apple-Fennel Slaw Fold a 36×18-inch sheet of heavy foil in half to make an 18-inch square. Cut 1 peeled tart apple into matchsticks, and cut 1 small fennel bulb into thin, bite-size strips. Place apple and fennel in the center of foil; top with 2 tablespoons sherry vinegar or balsamic vinegar, 1 tablespoon butter, 1 teaspoon packed brown sugar, dash salt, and dash cayenne pepper. Bring up two opposite edges of foil and seal with a double fold. Fold remaining ends to completely enclose slaw, leaving space for steam to build. Grill packet alongside patties 10 to 12 minutes or until fennel is tender.

PER SERVING 289 **CAL**; 18 g **FAT** (6 g **SAT**); 48 mg **CHOL**; 335 mg **SODIUM**; 19 g **CARB**; 1 g **FIBER**; 14 g **PRO**

Cubanitos

These diminutive versions of the wildly popular Cuban sandwich—roast pork, bacon or ham, dill pickles, Swiss cheese, and yellow mustard—are guaranteed to be gobbled up.

MAKES 16 servings **PREP** 20 minutes **COOK** 4 minutes

- 2 **tablespoons olive oil**
- 2 **cloves garlic, minced**
- 4 **ciabatta rolls, split**
- 2 **tablespoons yellow mustard**
- 8 **slices Swiss cheese**
- 8 **lengthwise slices sandwich dill pickles**
- 8 **ounces thinly sliced deli roast pork**
- 8 **slices packaged ready-to-serve cooked bacon, crisped according to package directions**

1 In a small bowl combine oil and garlic; set aside.

2 Trim tops and bottoms of ciabatta rolls to make flat surfaces. Brush outsides of rolls with oil mixture. Spread insides of rolls with mustard. Place one slice of the cheese on each roll bottom. Top with pickles. Divide pork among roll bottoms; top with bacon and the remaining four cheese slices. Replace roll tops.

3 Heat a large grill pan or skillet over medium heat. Add sandwiches. Weight with a heavy skillet. Cook 2 to 3 minutes or until bread is toasted. Turn sandwiches over, weight, and cook 2 to 3 minutes more or until bread is toasted and cheese is melted.

4 Cut each sandwich into four portions.

PER SERVING 117 **CAL**; 7 g **FAT** (3 g **SAT**); 26 mg **CHOL**; 234 mg **SODIUM**; 4 g **CARB**; 0 g **FIBER**; 9 g **PRO**

Cornmeal Griddle Cakes with Sautéed Corn

These sunny yellow griddle cakes make a lovely appetizer—or a side paired with roast chicken or grilled steak.

MAKES 15 servings **PREP** 30 minutes **COOK** 4 minutes per batch

4	**slices bacon**
1	**10-ounce package frozen whole kernel corn, thawed (2 cups)**
½	**cup chopped onion**
1	**cup buttermilk or sour milk***
1	**egg, lightly beaten**
1	**tablespoon snipped fresh chives**
¾	**cup all-purpose flour**
½	**cup blue or yellow cornmeal**
1	**tablespoon sugar**
1½	**teaspoons baking powder**
¼	**teaspoon baking soda**
¼	**teaspoon salt**
	Crème fraîche or sour cream
	Snipped fresh chives (optional)

1 In an extra-large skillet cook bacon until crisp. Remove bacon from skillet; reserving drippings in skillet. Drain bacon on paper towels and crumble finely; set aside.

2 Cook corn and onion in the reserved drippings over medium heat about 5 minutes or until corn and onion are tender. Cool slightly. Place half the corn mixture (about ¾ cup) in a food processor or blender. Cover and process or blend until nearly smooth. Transfer to a medium bowl. Stir in buttermilk, egg, and the 1 tablespoon chives.

3 In a large bowl, stir together flour, cornmeal, sugar, baking powder, baking soda, and salt. Add buttermilk mixture all at once to flour mixture. Stir just until moistened (batter should be slightly lumpy). Stir in the remaining corn mixture and bacon. Let batter stand 5 minutes.

4 Heat a lightly greased griddle or large heavy skillet over medium heat until a few drops of water dance across the surface. For each griddle cake, spoon a rounded tablespoon batter into skillet. Spread batter, if necessary, into a circle about 2 inches in diameter. Cook about 2 minutes on each side, turning when griddle cakes are golden brown and edges are slightly dry.

5 Serve warm with crème fraîche or sour cream. If desired, sprinkle with additional chives. Makes about 30 cakes.

*Tip To make 1 cup sour milk, place 1 tablespoon lemon juice or vinegar in a glass measure cup. Add enough milk to equal 1 cup total liquid; stir. Let stand 5 minutes before using in the recipe.

PER SERVING 389 **CAL**; 22 g **FAT** (10 g **SAT**); 81 mg **CHOL**; 492 mg **SODIUM**; 39 g **CARB**; 2 g **FIBER**; 10 g **PRO**

Grilled Vegetable Platter

These fresh, light, and gorgeous grilled veggies dressed with a lemony vinaigrette add balance to a spread of more indulgent appetizers.

MAKES 8 servings **PREP** 25 minutes **GRILL** 30 minutes

1	pound baby pattypan squash (about 3 cups)
2	medium yellow, orange, and/or red sweet peppers, seeded and cut into squares
12	ounces fresh green beans, trimmed (3 cups)
15	baby carrots with tops, trimmed
10	cherry sweet peppers
2	tablespoons olive oil or vegetable oil
½	teaspoon salt
¼	teaspoon black pepper
2	teaspoons finely shredded lemon peel
2	teaspoons lemon juice
2	cloves garlic, minced
	Nonstick cooking spray

1 In an extra-large bowl combine squash, sweet peppers, beans, carrots, cherry sweet peppers, oil, salt, and black pepper; toss to combine. For the dressing, in a small bowl stir together lemon peel, lemon juice, and garlic. Set aside.

2 Lightly coat an unheated grill wok with nonstick cooking spray; add vegetables. Grill, covered, over medium heat 30 to 35 minutes or until vegetables are crisp-tender and light brown, stirring occasionally.

3 Return cooked vegetables to the bowl. Add dressing; toss to coat. Serve on a large platter.

PER SERVING 75 **CAL**; 4 g **FAT** (1 g **SAT**); 0 mg **CHOL**; 289 mg **SODIUM**; 10 g **CARB**; 3 g **FIBER**; 2 g **PRO**

Cheddar-Beer Weenies

Keep these cheese-sauced cocktail weenies warm and ready to eat for up to 2 hours in the slow cooker.

MAKES 8 servings **PREP** 35 minutes **BAKE** 30 minutes
SLOW COOK 4 hours

1	**14- to 16-ounce package beef cocktail wieners**
12	**to 16 slices bacon, cut crosswise into thirds**
2	**tablespoons butter**
1	**cup finely chopped onion**
2	**cloves garlic, minced**
1	**cup beer**
½	**16-ounce jar (about ¾ cup) cheddar pasta sauce or one 10.75-ounce can condensed cheddar cheese soup**
1	**teaspoon hot pepper sauce**
½	**teaspoon chili powder**

1 Preheat oven to 400°F. Line a 15×10-inch baking pan with foil or parchment paper. Tightly wrap each cocktail wiener in a piece of bacon; secure with a wooden toothpick. Place in prepared pan. Bake 30 to 35 minutes or until bacon is browned and slightly crisp; cool slightly. Remove and discard toothpicks.

2 Meanwhile, for sauce, in a medium saucepan heat butter over medium heat until melted. Add onion and garlic; cook 5 to 8 minutes or until onion is tender, stirring occasionally. Remove from heat. Stir in beer, cheddar pasta sauce, hot pepper sauce, and chili powder.

3 In a 1½-quart slow cooker combine cocktail wieners and sauce. Cover and cook on low 4 to 5 hours or until heated. (If no heat setting is available, cook 3 to 4 hours.) Serve immediately or keep warm, covered, on warm or low up to 2 hours.

PER SERVING 500 **CAL**; 46 g **FAT** (18 g **SAT**); 88 mg **CHOL**; 1,211 mg **SODIUM**; 6 g **CARB**; 0 g **FIBER**; 14 g **PRO**

Sweet Potato Wedges with Hummus

While party snacks aren't usually expected to be healthful, these beta carotene-packed sweet potatoes dipped in high-fiber, high-protein hummus certainly are.

MAKES 8 servings **PREP** 30 minutes **BAKE** 25 minutes

5	**large sweet potatoes**
3	**tablespoons olive oil**
1	**teaspoon ground cumin**
½	**teaspoon salt**
½	**teaspoon garlic powder**
½	**teaspoon paprika**
1	**15-ounce can garbanzo beans (chickpeas), rinsed and drained**
⅓	**cup water**
3	**tablespoons lime or lemon juice**
3	**tablespoons tahini (sesame seed paste)**
2	**cloves garlic, minced**
1½	**teaspoons ground coriander**
1	**teaspoon cumin seeds, toasted (tip, page 8)**
½	**teaspoon cayenne pepper**
	Olive oil (optional)

1 Preheat oven to 450°F. Cut each sweet potato lengthwise into eight wedges. Place in an extra-large bowl. In a small bowl stir together oil, the ground cumin, the salt, and garlic powder. Drizzle over potato wedges; toss gently to coat.

2 Arrange potato wedges in a single layer on an extra-large baking sheet. Sprinkle with paprika. Bake 25 to 35 minutes or until potatoes are tender and lightly browned on the edges.

3 Meanwhile, for hummus, in a food processor combine the remaining ingredients except olive oil. Cover and process until smooth, scraping down sides of bowl as necessary. Transfer to a bowl; drizzle with olive oil, if desired, and serve with sweet potato wedges.

PER SERVING 242 **CAL**; 9 g **FAT** (1 g **SAT**); 0 mg **CHOL**; 368 mg **SODIUM**; 36 g **CARB**; 6 g **FIBER**; 6 g **PRO**

SWEET POTATO WEDGES
WITH HUMMUS

Savory Rosemary, Pancetta, and Fig Cheesecake

Heather Walker of Scottsdale, Arizona, won a big prize in a contest celebrating a big event—the 150th anniversary of Bertolli olive oils. Her savory appetizer cheesecake won her the 2015 grand prize—a trip for two to Tuscany that included a helicopter ride over the Italian countryside, a cooking class, and an expedition in search of the perfect truffle. It was the second international trip in a year for Heather, who has been entering cooking contests for 5 years. (The other was to Ireland, through the Ragland Road Irish Pub & Restaurant in Florida.) The stay-at-home mom says she tends to enter a lot of competitions in which the prize is travel in order to get out and about a bit. Sounds like it's working!

MAKES 18 servings   **PREP** 35 minutes   **STAND** 30 minutes   **BAKE** 30 minutes   **COOL** 1 hour   **COOK** 7 minutes

8	ounces cream cheese
4	ounces mascarpone cheese
3	egg whites
¼	cup Bertolli olive oil, plus 1 tablespoon
2	tablespoons chopped fresh rosemary
2	tablespoons whole wheat flour
2	teaspoons finely shredded lemon peel
¼	teaspoon salt
¼	teaspoon black pepper
2	tablespoons Bertolli olive oil, plus more for drizzling
4	ounces pancetta, chopped
½	cup chopped fresh figs*, plus 2 whole fresh figs to top the cheesecake, if desired
¼	cup pine nuts, toasted (tip, page 8)
¼	cup Bertolli balsamic vinegar
2	tablespoons brown sugar
1	tablespoon fresh thyme
¼	teaspoon salt
3	to 4 sprigs fresh thyme (optional)
	Buttery crackers

1 For the cheesecake, let cream cheese, mascarpone, and egg whites stand at room temperature 30 minutes.

2 Preheat oven to 350. Brush a 6×1½-inch cake pan with the 1 tablespoon olive oil. Line bottom and sides of pan with parchment paper. Place cake pan in a 2-quart baking dish; set aside. In a large bowl beat cream cheese and mascarpone cheese with a mixer on medium to high 30 seconds. Add ¼ cup olive oil, egg whites, rosemary, flour, lemon peel, salt, and pepper. Beat on high 2 minutes until light, creamy, and fluffy. Pour batter into cake pan. Pour boiling water into baking dish to reach halfway up sides of the cake pan.

3 Bake 30 minutes. Remove cheesecake from the water bath. Cool in the cake pan on a wire rack 1 hour. Using a butter knife, loosen edges of the cake from sides of pan. Remove cheesecake from the pan.

4 For the topping, in a large skillet heat the 2 tablespoons olive oil over medium heat. Add the pancetta and cook 3 minutes, stirring occasionally, until almost browned.

5 Add the chopped figs, pine nuts, balsamic vinegar, brown sugar, thyme, and salt. Bring to boiling. Reduce heat and simmer 4 to 5 minutes or until vinegar mixture is reduced and caramelized.

6 Remove topping from heat and pour it over the top of the cheesecake. Lightly drizzle with olive oil just before serving.

7 If desired, cut the whole fresh figs in half and place them on the cheesecake. Top with additional thyme sprigs. Serve with buttery crackers.

*Tip When fresh figs are unavailable, reconstitute dried figs by placing them in a container and adding water to cover the fruit. Cover and refrigerate for 8 hours; drain.

PER SERVING 173 **CAL**; 16 g **FAT** (6 g **SAT**); 27 mg **CHOL**; 217 mg **SODIUM**; 5 g **CARB**; 0 g **FIBER**; 23 g **PRO**

Cheesy Skillet Artichoke Dip

The dippers—two-bite-size rolls—are baked right on top of the creamy dip in this supremely popular party dish.

MAKES 24 servings **PREP** 30 minutes **RISE** 1 hour **BAKE** 30 minutes **STAND** 10 minutes

1	**15- to 16-ounce package frozen white dinner rolls, thawed (12 rolls)**
1	**8-ounce package cream cheese, softened**
1	**8-ounce carton sour cream**
¼	**cup milk**
2	**cups shredded Italian blend cheeses**
2	**14-ounce cans artichoke hearts, drained and chopped**
3	**cups chopped fresh baby spinach**
½	**cup sliced green onions**
2	**cloves garlic, minced**
1	**tablespoon butter, melted**
1	**tablespoon grated Parmesan cheese**

1 Divide each roll into two portions. Shape each portion into a small ball, pulling edges under to make a smooth top. Place rolls 2 to 3 inches apart on a floured sheet of parchment paper or waxed paper. Lightly cover and let rise 1 to 1½ hours or until nearly double in size.

2 Preheat oven to 375°F. In an extra-large bowl beat cream cheese with a mixer on medium to high 30 seconds. Add sour cream and milk; beat until combined. Beat in 1½ cups of the shredded cheeses. Stir in artichokes, spinach, green onions, and garlic. Transfer dip to an extra-large oven-going skillet, spreading evenly. Sprinkle remaining shredded cheeses over dip.

3 Bake 15 minutes. Remove skillet from oven.

4 Place rolls on hot dip (rolls will fit snugly and cover entire surface). Lightly brush roll tops with melted butter then sprinkle Parmesan cheese. Bake 15 to 20 minutes more or until rolls are golden and dip is hot. Let stand 10 minutes before serving.

PER SERVING 147 **CAL**; 8 g **FAT** (5 g **SAT**); 24 mg **CHOL**; 242 mg **SODIUM**; 13 g **CARB**; 1 g **FIBER**; 5 g **PRO**

Cucumber-Feta Dip

With its colorful garnish of bright-green mint leaves and ruby-red pomegranate seeds, this light and healthful dip based on Greek yogurt and light sour cream is perfect for the winter holidays. Serve with raw veggies or thin crackers.

MAKES 9 servings **PREP** 20 minutes **CHILL** 2 hours

1	**cup plain Greek yogurt**
½	**cup light sour cream**
½	**cup crumbled feta cheese**
¼	**cup finely chopped red onion**
1	**tablespoon lemon juice**
½	**teaspoon salt**
2	**cups coarsely shredded English cucumber**
	Pomegranate seeds (optional)
	Snipped fresh mint leaves (optional)

1 In a medium bowl combine yogurt, sour cream, feta cheese, onion, lemon juice, and salt. Chill, covered, 2 to 8 hours.

2 Before serving, place shredded cucumber in a fine-mesh sieve. Use the back of a large spoon or a rubber spatula to press cucumber to remove excess liquid. Stir cucumber into dip. Sprinkle with pomegranate seeds and snipped fresh mint, if desired.

PER SERVING 68 **CAL**; 4 g **FAT** (3 g **SAT**); 14 mg **CHOL**; 239 mg **SODIUM**; 4 g **CARB**; 0 g **FIBER**; 4 g **PRO**

Avocado Deviled Eggs

Don't skip the step of tossing the avocado pieces with the lemon juice. It prevents the avocado from turning brown.

MAKES 24 servings **PREP** 45 minutes **CHILL** 4 hours

12	**eggs**
½	**cup mayonnaise**
1	**tablespoon country Dijon mustard**
1	**teaspoon caper juice or sweet or dill pickle juice**
⅛	**teaspoon freshly ground black pepper**
	Dash bottled hot pepper sauce
1	**ripe but firm avocado, halved, seeded, and peeled**
1	**teaspoon lemon juice**
	Snipped fresh chives (optional)

1 Place eggs in a single layer in a large Dutch oven. Add enough cold water to cover the eggs by at least 1 inch. Bring to a rapid boil over high heat (water will have large rapidly breaking bubbles). Remove from heat. Cover and let stand 15 minutes; drain. Run cold water over the eggs or place them in ice water until cool enough to handle; drain. Peel eggs and cut in half lengthwise. Remove yolks and place in a large bowl. Set whites aside.

2 Mash egg yolks with a fork. Stir in mayonnaise, mustard, caper juice, black pepper, and hot pepper sauce.

3 Chop avocados to ½-inch pieces; toss with lemon juice. Spoon or pipe egg yolk mixture into egg white halves. Place pieces of avocado on top. If desired, sprinkle with chives. Cover and chill up to 4 hours before serving.

PER SERVING 79 **CAL**; 7 g **FAT** (1 g **SAT**); 95 mg **CHOL**; 73 mg **SODIUM**; 1 g **CARB**; 0 g **FIBER**; 3 g **PRO**

Cheese Wafers with Pepper Jelly

There's something magical about the combination of the sweet-spicy jelly rich and the buttery crackers flavored with sharp cheddar, curry powder, and cayenne.

MAKES 20 servings **PREP** 15 minutes **CHILL** 2 hours **BAKE** 8 minutes per batch

- **2**   **cups all-purpose flour**
- **½**   **cup butter, cut up**
- **1**   **teaspoon sugar**
- **¼**   **teaspoon salt**
- **¼**   **teaspoon curry powder**
       Dash cayenne pepper
- **2**   **cups shredded sharp cheddar cheese (8 ounces)**
- **4**   **to 5 tablespoons water**
       Jalapeño pepper jelly

1 In a food processor combine flour, butter, sugar, salt, curry powder, and cayenne pepper. Cover and process with two or three pulses until pieces are pea size. Add cheese. Cover and process with two or three pulses until mixed. Add the water, 1 tablespoon at a time, pulsing after each addition just until mixture is moistened.

2 Gather cheese mixture into a ball; divide dough in half. Shape each half into a 10-inch roll. Wrap in plastic wrap and chill for 2 to 24 hours.

3 Preheat oven to 400°F. Grease a large baking sheet or line with parchment paper. Cut rolls into ¼-inch slices. Place slices 1 inch apart on the prepared baking sheet. Prick slices with a fork.

4 Bake 8 to 10 minutes or until edges just start to brown. Transfer to a wire rack to cool. Serve with jalapeño pepper jelly.

PER SERVING 170 **CAL**; 9 g **FAT** (5 g **SAT**); 24 mg **CHOL**; 143 mg **SODIUM**; 20 g **CARB**; 0 g **FIBER**; 4 g **PRO**

Chile Pecans

Of the three types that are options in this recipe, the ancho chile pepper is probably the easiest to find. Ancho chiles are dried poblano peppers. They have a rich, sweet raisin-like flavor with just a little heat.

MAKES 10 servings   **PREP** 15 minutes   **BAKE** 45 minutes

- **2**   **cups pecan halves**
- **2**   **tablespoons coffee liqueur or maple syrup**
- **4**   **teaspoons vegetable oil**
- **2**   **tablespoons sugar**
- **2**   **tablespoons ground Chimayo, ancho, or pasilla chile pepper**

1 Preheat oven to 250°F. Line a 13×9-inch baking pan with foil; set aside. In a medium bowl combine pecan halves, liqueur, and oil. Stir in sugar and chile pepper. Spread in prepared pan.

2 Bake, uncovered, 45 minutes, stirring twice. Spread on a large piece of foil to cool. Store in airtight container at room temperature up to 2 weeks or freeze up to 1 month.

PER SERVING 192 **CAL**; 18 g **FAT** (2 g **SAT**); 0 mg **CHOL**; 16 mg **SODIUM**; 8 g **CARB**; 3 g **FIBER**; 2 g **PRO**

Cinnamon Pretzels

Fans of salty-sweet flavors will love these sugar- and cinnamon-coated pretzels. They're equally good with a cold beer or a cup of hot chocolate.

MAKES 12 servings **PREP** 10 minutes **BAKE** 30 minutes

⅔ **cup vegetable oil**
½ **cup sugar**
2 **teaspoons ground cinnamon**
1 **1-pound package small pretzel twists**

1 Preheat oven to 300°F*. In a large roasting pan stir together oil, sugar, and cinnamon. Add pretzels; toss well to combine. Bake, uncovered, 30 minutes, stirring twice. Spread pretzels on a large sheet of waxed paper to cool.

* To make in a microwave, in an extra-large bowl stir together oil, sugar, and cinnamon. Add pretzels; toss to coat. Place half the pretzels in a large microwave-safe bowl. Microwave on high 3 minutes, stirring after every minute. Spread pretzels on a large sheet of waxed paper to cool. Repeat with remaining pretzels.

PER SERVING 287 **CAL**; 13 g **FAT** (1 g **SAT**); 0 mg **CHOL**; 547 mg **SODIUM**; 38 g **CARB**; 2 g **FIBER**; 3 g **PRO**

bring on breakfast

Good mornings start with something good to eat. Find recipes here!

GRANDMA'S APPLE GRUFF-IN

Shakshuka with Deep Fried Garlic

Winning cooking contests is nothing new to Jodi Taffel (a.k.a. "The Fabulous Bacon Babe") of Altadena, California. She is a five-time award winner at The Grilled Cheese Invitational and a two-time Top-10 finisher at The World Food Championships. But winning 1st prize at the Gilroy Garlic Festival—which she did in 2015 with this hearty dish of eggs baked in a highly spiced tomato sauce—was "number one on my bucket list." The tipping point for the judges surely must have been the crispy deep-fried garlic garnish.

MAKES 7 servings **PREP** 45 minutes **COOK** 1 hour **BAKE** 15 minutes

½ **pound bacon, coarsely chopped (about 10 slices)**
1 **cup chopped onion**
1 **cup large chopped red sweet pepper**
3 **tablespoons large minced shallot**
¼ **cup pickled jalapeño peppers, chopped**
2 **tablespoons minced garlic**
2 **tablespoons grated fresh ginger**
1 **tablespoon chopped canned chipotle in adobo sauce (tip, page 11)**
1 **tablespoon Asian chile paste (sambal oelek)**
1 **28-ounce can whole peeled tomatoes**
¼ **cup honey**
2 **tablespoons dried tarragon**
1 **tablespoon paprika**
1 **tablespoon cumin**
2 **cups spinach**
1 **cup crumbled feta cheese plus 2 tablespoons**
7 **extra-large eggs**
1 **recipe Deep Fried Garlic**
¼ **cup chopped green onions**
   Barberi or pita bread

1 Preheat oven to 400°F. For the sauce, in a large saucepan cook bacon over medium heat until crisp. Remove bacon with a slotted spoon; set aside. Drain all but 1 tablespoon fat from the pan.

2 Add onion, sweet pepper, and shallot to pan. Cook over medium heat 6 to 8 minutes or until tender. Add jalapeños, garlic, ginger, chipotle pepper, and Asian chile paste. Cook 1 to 2 minutes or until fragrant.

3 Crush undrained tomatoes with your hands. Add to sauce in pan. Bring to a boil. Reduce heat and simmer 5 minutes, stirring occasionally.

4 Add honey, tarragon, paprika, and cumin. Simmer, covered, 20 minutes. Remove from heat. Stir in spinach and bacon.

5 Divide 1 cup of the feta between seven 8- to 10-ounce individual casserole dishes. Add about ⅔ cup sauce to each casserole. Make a depression in the middle of sauce. One at a time, crack eggs into a ramekin then slide into the depression in the sauce. Sprinkle with remaining feta.

6 Place casseroles on a baking sheet. Bake 15 to 18 minutes or until eggs are desired doneness.

7 Sprinkle casseroles with a few cloves of the Deep Fried Garlic and green onions. Serve with barberi.

Deep Fried Garlic Place 14 garlic cloves in a small saucepan. Add 1½ cups whole milk; bring to a boil. Reduce heat and simmer, uncovered, 20 minutes or until garlic cloves are softened; drain. In a small heavy saucepan heat 2 cups olive oil to 350°F. Place ¼ cup flour in a small bowl. Place 1 extra-large egg and 1 teaspoon water in another small bowl and beat slightly. Place ¼ cup bread crumbs in a third bowl. Working in batches, coat 3 or 4 garlic cloves in flour, then egg mixture, then bread crumbs. Fry in hot oil 15 to 20 seconds or until cloves are golden brown.

PER SERVING 492 **CAL**; 18 g **FAT** (7 g **SAT**); 239 mg **CHOL**; 1,101 mg **SODIUM**; 60 g **CARB**; 6 g **FIBER**; 23 g **PRO**

Kettle Chip Frittata with Bacon, Cheddar, and Arugula

Many breakfast and brunch dishes feature potatoes—but this one is unique with crunchy potato chips baked right into the egg mixture. It makes a fun supper dish too.

MAKES 6 servings **PREP** 20 minutes **BAKE** 50 minutes **STAND** 10 minutes

10	eggs
¾	cup whole milk
1	teaspoon kosher salt
¼	teaspoon cayenne pepper
3	cups kettle cooked potato chips
3	cups fresh arugula, shredded
1½	cups shredded sharp cheddar cheese
1½	cups cherry tomatoes, halved
10	strips bacon, coarsely chopped, crisp-cooked, and drained
¼	cup snipped fresh basil

1 Preheat oven to 350°F. Lightly grease a 2-quart baking dish; set aside. In a large bowl whisk together eggs and milk. Add salt and cayenne. Gently fold in the potato chips, making sure they are completely covered by the egg mixture. Stir in arugula, cheese, cherry tomatoes, bacon, and basil. Transfer to the prepared baking dish.

2 Bake 50 minutes until golden brown and a knife inserted near the center comes out clean. Let stand 10 to 15 minutes.

PER SERVING 410 **CAL**; 29 g **FAT** (11 g **SAT**); 357 mg **CHOL**; 1,001 mg **SODIUM**; 13 g **CARB**; 1 g **FIBER**; 25 g **PRO**

Ham-and-Cheese-Stuffed French Toast

For fans of salty-sweet flavors, this French toast with ham and cheese in the middle and maple syrup drizzled over the top is a sublime way to start the day.

MAKES 6 servings **START TO FINISH** 25 minutes

2	eggs
1	cup half-and-half or light cream
1	teaspoon vanilla
½	teaspoon ground cinnamon
½	pound cooked, shaved brown sugar-cured ham
12	very thin slices Swiss cheese (about 6 ounces)
12	thin slices firm-texture white bread
	Butter
¼	cup sliced almonds, lightly toasted*
	Sifted powdered sugar
	Maple syrup

1 In a medium bowl beat eggs, half-and-half, vanilla, and cinnamon until well mixed. Pour into a shallow pan or dish.

2 For each sandwich, tuck a generous amount of ham between two slices of cheese; place between two slices of the white bread.

3 Dip sandwiches in egg mixture. Cook on a hot buttered griddle or nonstick skillet until golden, turning once.

4 Cut each sandwich in half diagonally and arrange on six plates. Sprinkle with almonds and sifted powdered sugar. Pass maple syrup.

*Tip To toast whole nuts or large pieces, spread them in a shallow pan. Bake in a 350°F oven 5 to 10 minutes, shaking the pan once or twice. Toast coconut in the same way, watching it closely to prevent burning.

PER SERVING 461 **CAL**; 23 g **FAT** (11 g **SAT**); 127 mg **CHOL**; 760 mg **SODIUM**; 43 g **CARB**; 1 g **FIBER**; 23 g **PRO**

Hash Browns Taco

You can substitute a 20-ounce package of prepared frozen hash browns, thawed, for the homemade version, if you like. When making them from scratch, it's important to get the shredded potatoes as dry as possible before frying them in order to get a crispy crust and tender interior.

MAKES 4 servings **START TO FINISH** 40 minutes

1	recipe Perfect Hash Browns
4	ounces ground beef or bulk pork sausage
½	cup purchased salsa
¼	cup frozen whole kernel corn
2	eggs
2	tablespoons milk
⅛	teaspoon salt
1	tablespoon butter
½	cup shredded cheddar or Monterey Jack cheese with jalapeño chile peppers (2 ounces)
1	roma tomato, chopped
2	tablespoons thinly sliced green onion
1	avocado, seeded, peeled, and thinly sliced (optional)
	Sour cream (optional)

1 Prepare Perfect Hash Browns; keep warm.

2 In a medium skillet cook ground beef over medium heat. Drain off fat. Stir salsa and corn into meat in skillet. Bring to boiling; reduce heat. Simmer, uncovered, 5 minutes.

3 In a small bowl beat together eggs, milk, and salt with a whisk or fork. In a small skillet melt butter over medium heat; pour in egg mixture. Cook over medium heat, without stirring, until mixture begins to set on the bottom and around edges. With a spatula or a large spoon, lift and fold the partially cooked egg mixture so the uncooked portion flows underneath. Continue cooking over medium heat 2 to 3 minutes or until egg mixture is cooked through, but is still glossy and moist. Immediately remove from heat.

4 Spoon meat filling over half of the hash browns; sprinkle with cheese. Top with scrambled eggs. Fold the other half of the hash browns over the filling. In a small bowl combine tomato and green onion. Serve taco with tomato relish and, if desired, avocado and sour cream.

Perfect Hash Browns Peel and coarsely shred 1¼ pounds russet potatoes. Place potatoes in a large bowl; add enough water to cover potatoes. Stir well. Drain in a colander set over the sink. Repeat rinsing and draining two or three times until water runs clear. Drain again, pressing out as much water as you can with a rubber spatula. Line a salad spinner with paper towels; add potatoes and spin. Repeat, if necessary, until potatoes are dry. Transfer potatoes to a large bowl. Sprinkle with ¼ teaspoon salt and ⅛ teaspoon black pepper; toss to combine. In a large nonstick skillet heat 1 tablespoon olive oil and 1 tablespoon butter over medium-high heat until butter foams. Add potatoes to the skillet, spreading into an even layer. Gently press with the back of a spatula to form a cake. Reduce heat to medium. Cook, without stirring, 12 minutes or until the bottom is golden brown and crisp. Invert a plate over the top of the skillet. Carefully invert skillet to transfer the potatoes to the plate. If needed, add 1 tablespoon olive oil to skillet. Using the plate, slide potatoes back into the skillet, uncooked side down. Cook 8 minutes or until the bottom is golden brown.

PER SERVING 372 **CAL**; 21 g **FAT** (10 g **SAT**); 143 mg **CHOL**; 617 mg **SODIUM**; 31 g **CARB**; 3 g **FIBER**; 16 g **PRO**

For Goodness Cake! Breakfast Cupcakes

When you can't decide what to have for breakfast, you can have it all in these indulgent "cupcakes" built from layers of mini waffles, savory sausage, eggs, cheese—and creamy maple syrup-infused cream cheese frosting. Ronna Farley of Rockville, Maryland, won the grand prize in the 2014 Jones Dairy Farm "Rise, Sizzle, and Shine" recipe contest with this hybrid recipe that was picked by Jones Dairy Farm Facebook fans from among the 280 entries. "I have always loved Jones sausage links," Ronna says, "and it was a joy to create a new, exciting breakfast recipe."

MAKES 12 servings   **PREP** 15 minutes   **BAKE** 18 minutes   **COOL** 5 minutes

	Nonstick cooking spray
12	**frozen mini waffles, thawed**
1	**7-ounce package Jones Dairy Farm All Natural Golden Brown Sausage Links, thawed and sliced**
6	**eggs, lightly beaten**
1	**8-ounce package shredded cheddar cheese**
½	**cup ricotta cheese**
¼	**teaspoon salt**
⅓	**cup butter, softened**
6	**ounces cream cheese, softened**
2½	**cups powdered sugar**
2	**tablespoons pure maple syrup**

1 Preheat oven to 375°F. Lightly coat twelve 2½-inch muffin cups with cooking spray.

2 Lightly toast waffles. Place one waffle in each prepared muffin cup. Top with sausage pieces.

3 In a large bowl combine eggs, cheddar cheese, ricotta cheese, and salt. Spoon over sausage pieces.

4 Bake 18 minutes or until cupcakes are set and golden brown. Cool in pan on wire rack 5 minutes. Run knife around edge of each cupcake; remove from pan.

5 In a medium bowl beat butter and cream cheese with a mixer on medium until fluffy. Gradually beat in powdered sugar and maple syrup until smooth. Pipe or spread frosting over cupcakes. Serve immediately.

PER SERVING 418 **CAL**; 27 g **FAT** (14 g **SAT**); 159 mg **CHOL**; 450 mg **SODIUM**; 32 g **CARB**; 0 g **FIBER**; 12 g **PRO**

Savory Brunch Muffins

Smoked salmon, dill, and hard-cooked eggs give flavor and heft to these buttermilk muffins. A crispy crown of crushed potato chips serves as a savory "streusel" topping.

MAKES 12 servings **PREP** 20 minutes **BAKE** 15 minutes **COOL** 5 minutes

2	cups all-purpose flour
1	tablespoon sugar
1½	teaspoons baking powder
½	teaspoon baking soda
¼	teaspoon salt
½	cup buttermilk
½	cup sour cream
2	eggs
3	tablespoons butter, melted
2	tablespoons snipped fresh dill
2	ounces smoked salmon (lox-style), chopped
2	hard-cooked eggs, peeled and chopped
1	cup wavy potato chips, crushed

1 Preheat oven to 400°F. Grease twelve 2½-inch muffin cups or line cups with parchment paper squares*; set aside. In a large bowl stir together flour, sugar, baking powder, baking soda, and salt. Make a well in the center of flour mixture.

2 In a 2-cup measure whisk together buttermilk, sour cream, eggs, butter, and dill. Add all at once to flour mixture. Gently stir just until moistened (batter should be lumpy). Gently fold in salmon and chopped eggs.

3 Spoon batter into prepared muffin cups, filling each three-fourths full. Sprinkle crushed potato chips over batter in cups. Bake 15 minutes or until golden. Cool in cups on a wire rack 5 minutes.

* To make parchment cups, cut parchment paper into 5-inch squares. Spray each muffin cup with nonstick cooking spray then press a parchment square into each cup, pressing paper firmly against the sides to pleat. (The parchment will be loose until batter is added.)

PER SERVING 169 **CAL**; 7 g **FAT** (3 g **SAT**); 75 mg **CHOL**; 335 mg **SODIUM**; 19 g **CARB**; 1 g **FIBER**; 6 g **PRO**

Potatoes with Chorizo

This simple and hearty dish is a bit like a chunky hash. Serve it for brunch with a fresh fruit salad—or for a quick supper with a crisp green salad.

MAKES 6 servings **START TO FINISH** 45 minutes

- **1   pound tiny new potatoes**
- **2   tablespoons water**
- **8   ounces uncooked Mexican chorizo,* casings removed if present**
- **⅓   cup chopped onion**
- **½   cup chopped red and/or yellow sweet pepper**
- **½   teaspoon ground cumin**
-     **Black pepper**

1 Cut potatoes in half. Cut each half into thirds to form uniform bite-size pieces. Place potatoes in a single layer in a microwave-safe baking dish; add the water. Cook, loosely covered, on high 8 minutes or until potatoes are tender, stirring once. (Or in a large covered saucepan cook potatoes in enough boiling salted water to cover 10 minutes or until tender.) Drain and set aside.

2 In a large skillet cook chorizo over medium-high heat until no longer pink, using a wooden spoon to break up meat as it cooks. Using a slotted spoon, remove chorizo and drain on paper towels, reserving 1 tablespoon drippings in skillet. Pat chorizo with paper towels to remove additional fat.

3 Add onion to the reserved drippings; cook 1 minute. Add cooked potatoes, sweet pepper, and cumin. Cook 8 minutes or until potatoes are golden brown and vegetables are tender, stirring frequently. Stir in cooked chorizo; heat through. Season to taste with black pepper.

*Tip Mexican chorizo is made from ground fatty pork and seasoned with chile peppers. You can find it with or without casings. Spanish chorizo is generally a cured smoked sausage seasoned with pimiento.

PER SERVING 235 **CAL**; 15 g **FAT** (5 g **SAT**); 33 mg **CHOL**; 473 mg **SODIUM**; 15 g **CARB**; 2 g **FIBER**; 11 g **PRO**

Grandma's Apple Gruff-In

So what is a gruff-in, anyway? Susan Datte of Freeland, Michigan, who won the Desserts category in the 2014 Michigan Apple Recipe Contest with this recipe, says that she was always told growing up that it means "apples are punched into the pastry". Susan's grandmother and mother were both great bakers. "When we were kids, my mom would make it and say, 'It's just like Grandma's.' It makes me feel very nostalgic. When I make it I know my mom and grandma are here with me."

MAKES 16 servings **PREP** 40 minutes **STAND** 20 minutes **RISE** 1 hour **BAKE** 48 minutes

2½ to 2¾ cups all-purpose flour
½   cup Pioneer sugar
1   package Fleischmann's active dry yeast
½   teaspoon salt
½   teaspoon Meyer lemon zest or regular lemon
½   cup evaporated milk
¼   cup water
¼   cup butter
2   ounces cream cheese
½   cup instant mashed potatoes
2   eggs
3   Michigan Northern Spy or Ida Red apples, peeled, cored, and sliced
½   cup walnuts, chopped
1   tablespoon Meyer lemon juice or regular lemon
½   teaspoon ground cinnamon
1   recipe Powdered Sugar Icing

1 In a large bowl combine 1 cup of the flour, 2 tablespoons of the sugar, yeast, salt, and lemon zest. In a small saucepan combine evaporated milk, the water, butter, cream cheese, and instant potatoes. Cook and stir over low heat just until warm (120°F to 130°F). Butter does not need to melt and mixture will be thick.

2 Add potato mixture to flour mixture. Beat with a mixer on medium 2 minutes. Add eggs and ½ cup of the flour; mix well. Stir in as much of the remaining flour as you can. Turn dough out onto a lightly floured surface. Knead in enough of the remaining flour to make a moderately stiff dough that is smooth and elastic (3 to 5 minutes total). Shape into a ball. Place in a lightly greased bowl. Cover and let rest 20 minutes.

3 Meanwhile, in a medium bowl combine apples, walnuts, the remaining 6 tablespoons sugar, lemon juice, and cinnamon. Set aside.

4 Turn dough out onto a heavily floured surface. Roll out dough to a 14-inch circle. Place dough on a pizza stone or 14-inch pizza pan. Arrange about two-thirds of the apple slices in a circle about 1 inch from the edge of the dough. Arrange remaining one-third of the apple slices in a circle inside the larger circle. Sprinkle with walnuts remaining in the bowl. Cover and let rise about 1 hour or until doubled in size.

5 Preheat oven to 350°F. Place gruff-in on an oven rack positioned over a large baking sheet on the rack below. Bake 48 to 50 minutes or until golden brown and a thermometer inserted in the center registers 190°F. Loosely cover with foil the last 15 minutes of baking to prevent overbrowning. Cool slightly.

6 Before serving, drizzle Powdered Sugar Icing over gruff-in.

Powdered Sugar Icing Stir together 1 cup powdered sugar, 1 tablespoon milk, and ¼ teaspoon vanilla. Stir in additional milk, 1 teaspoon at a time, until spreading consistency.

PER SERVING 234 CAL; 8 g FAT (3 g SAT); 37 mg CHOL; 130 mg SODIUM; 37 g CARB; 2 g FIBER; 5 g PRO

Maple Bacon Scones

These scones—featuring the favorite flavor combination of sweet maple syrup with smoky, salty bacon—are the type of scone you nibble with a cup of coffee, rather than with the more traditional pot of tea.

MAKES 12 servings **PREP** 25 minutes **BAKE** 13 minutes

1½ **cups all-purpose flour**
½ **cup whole wheat flour**
1½ **teaspoons baking powder**
¼ **teaspoon baking soda**
¼ **teaspoon salt**
¼ **cup cold butter, cut up**
3 **tablespoons plain Greek fat-free yogurt**
2 **eggs, lightly beaten, or ½ cup refrigerated or frozen egg product, thawed**
¼ **cup buttermilk**
¼ **cup light pancake syrup**
½ **teaspoon maple flavoring**
2 **slices thick-cut bacon, crisp-cooked, drained, and finely chopped**
   Buttermilk
⅓ **cup powdered sugar**
2 **teaspoons fat-free milk**
½ **teaspoon maple flavoring**

1 Preheat oven to 400°F. In a large bowl stir together all-purpose flour, whole wheat flour, baking powder, baking soda, and salt. Using a pastry blender, cut in butter until mixture resembles coarse crumbs. Add yogurt and toss until combined. Make a well in the center of the flour mixture.

2 In a small bowl combine eggs, ¼ cup buttermilk, the syrup, and ½ teaspoon maple flavoring. Stir in the bacon. Add buttermilk mixture all at once to flour mixture. Stir just until moistened.

3 Turn dough out onto a lightly floured surface. Knead dough by folding and gently pressing it for 10 to 12 strokes or until nearly smooth. Pat or lightly roll dough into an 8-inch circle about ¾ inch thick. Brush top with additional buttermilk. Using a floured knife, cut circle into 12 wedges.

4 Place dough wedges 2 inches apart on an ungreased baking sheet. Bake 13 to 15 minutes or until edges are lightly browned.

5 For glaze, in a small bowl stir together powdered sugar, fat-free milk, and ½ teaspoon maple flavoring. Add more milk if needed to make glaze drizzling consistency. Drizzle over warm scones.

PER SERVING 157 **CAL**; 6 g **FAT** (3 g **SAT**); 43 mg **CHOL**; 247 mg **SODIUM**; 22 g **CARB**; 1 g **FIBER**; 5 g **PRO**

Chocolate-Caramel Monkey Bread

If this ooey, gooey breakfast bread could get any better, this version accomplishes it. Cocoa powder and chocolate-covered caramels take it over the top!

MAKES 16 servings **PREP** 40 minutes **BAKE** 40 minutes **COOL** 5 minutes

½   cup sliced almonds or chopped pecans, toasted (tip, page 31)
¾   cup sugar
2   teaspoons unsweetened cocoa powder
1½   teaspoons ground cinnamon
2   16.3-ounce packages refrigerated biscuits (16 total)
32   chocolate-covered caramels (such as Rolo)
½   cup butter, melted
¼   cup caramel-flavor ice cream topping
1   teaspoon vanilla

1 Preheat oven to 350°F. Generously grease a 10-inch nonstick fluted tube pan. Sprinkle ¼ cup of the almonds in bottom of pan. In a small bowl combine sugar, cocoa powder, and cinnamon.

2 With kitchen scissors, cut each biscuit into two pieces. Using your hands, flatten each piece into a 3-inch round. Place a chocolate-covered caramel in the center of each round. Bring the edge of the dough up and around the caramel to form a ball. Pinch edges of dough together to seal firmly.

3 Dip each ball into the melted butter, then roll it in the sugar mixture. Layer coated balls in the prepared pan. Drizzle with any remaining butter; sprinkle with any remaining sugar mixture.

4 Stir together ice cream topping and vanilla; drizzle over rolls. Sprinkle with the remaining ¼ cup almonds.

5 Bake 40 to 45 minutes or until a toothpick comes out clean; cover bread with foil the last 15 minutes of baking to prevent overbrowning. Cool bread in pan 5 minutes. Run a small rubber spatula around edge of the bread to loosen. Invert onto a platter. Spoon topping and nuts in pan on bread. Cool slightly. Serve warm.

PER SERVING 347 **CAL**; 17 g **FAT** (7 g **SAT**); 17 mg **CHOL**; 658 mg **SODIUM**; 47 g **CARB**; 1 g **FIBER**; 4 g **PRO**

Pumpkin Coffee Break Cake

This beautiful Bundt cake draped in a yummy orange glaze is the perfect treat for a fall brunch.

MAKES 16 servings **PREP** 30 minutes **BAKE** 45 minutes **COOL** 2 hours + 20 minutes

Nonstick cooking spray
- 1 **cup all-purpose flour**
- 1 **cup white whole wheat flour**
- 2½ **teaspoons baking powder**
- 2 **teaspoons pumpkin pie spice or 1 teaspoon ground cinnamon, ½ teaspoon ground nutmeg, and ¼ teaspoon ground ginger**
- 1 **teaspoon finely shredded orange peel**
- ½ **teaspoon salt**
- 1 **cup water**
- ¾ **cup canned pumpkin**
- 1 **cup sugar**
- ¼ **cup canola oil**
- 1 **teaspoon vanilla, butter, and nut flavoring or 2 teaspoons vanilla**
- 4 **egg whites or ½ cup refrigerated or frozen egg product, thawed**
- ¾ **cup chopped pecans, toasted (tip, page 31)**
- ½ **cup orange juice**
- 2 **tablespoons sugar**
- 1½ **teaspoons cornstarch**
- ¼ **teaspoon vanilla, butter, and nut flavoring or ½ teaspoon vanilla**

1 For cake, preheat oven to 325°F. Generously coat a 10-inch nonstick fluted tube pan with cooking spray; set aside. In a medium bowl combine all-purpose flour, white whole wheat flour, baking powder, pumpkin pie spice, orange peel, and salt; set aside. In a small bowl combine the water and pumpkin.

2 In a large bowl combine the 1 cup sugar, oil, and 1 teaspoon flavoring. Beat with a mixer on medium-high until well mixed. Add egg whites, one at a time, beating well after each addition. Alternately add flour mixture and pumpkin mixture to beaten mixture, beating on low after each addition just until combined.

3 Sprinkle pecans in the bottom of the prepared tube pan. Carefully pour batter evenly over pecans. Bake 45 to 50 minutes or until a wooden pick inserted in center of cake comes out clean. Cool in pan on a wire rack 20 minutes. Invert pan and cake together. Remove pan. Cool cake on wire rack at least 2 hours.

4 Meanwhile, for glaze, in a small saucepan combine orange juice, the 2 tablespoons sugar, and the cornstarch; stir until cornstarch is completely dissolved. Cook and stir over medium-high heat until boiling; cook and stir 1 minute more. Remove from heat. Stir in the ¼ teaspoon flavoring. Cool completely.

5 Just before serving, drizzle cooled glaze over cooled cake.

PER SERVING 189 **CAL**; 7 g **FAT** (1 g **SAT**); 0 mg **CHOL**; 164 mg **SODIUM**; 29 g **CARB**; 2 g **FIBER**; 3 g **PRO**

Blueberry-Peach Gratin

There's a surprise at the bottom of each of these individual warm fruit gratins—crushed gingersnaps! This recipe makes a lovely dish for a brunch or a healthful dessert after a heavy meal.

MAKES 6 servings   **PREP** 20 minutes   **BROIL** 7 minutes

16	gingersnaps, crushed
2	cups peeled and chopped fresh peaches or frozen unsweetened peach slices, thawed and chopped
2	cups fresh blueberries
1	5.3- to 6-ounce honey-flavor fat-free Greek yogurt
2	tablespoons honey
2	teaspoons lemon juice
¼	cup powdered sugar (optional)

1 Preheat broiler. Butter six 10-ounce ramekins. Divide crushed gingersnaps among prepared ramekins. Top with peaches and blueberries.

2 In a small bowl combine yogurt, honey, and lemon juice. Spread mixture evenly over fruit in ramekins.

3 Place ramekins in a shallow baking pan. Broil 4 inches from heat 7 to 9 minutes or until blueberries begin to burst. Serve immediately. If desired, dust with powdered sugar.

PER SERVING 169 **CAL**; 2 g **FAT**; (0 g **SAT**); 0 mg **CHOL**; 105 mg **SODIUM**; 35 g **CARB**; 2 g **FIBER**; 4 g **PRO**

Coconut Granola

Full of all kinds of good things—including toasted oats, coconut, sunflower seeds, sesame seeds, and dried fruit—this crunchy granola is wonderful in a bowl with milk or sprinkled over yogurt or ice cream.

MAKES 34 servings **PREP** 20 minutes **BAKE** 45 minutes

2½ **cups rolled oats**
1½ **cups flaked or shredded coconut**
¼ **cup shelled sunflower seeds**
¼ **cup sesame seeds**
¼ **cup butter**
¼ **cup packed brown sugar**
¼ **cup honey or agave nectar**
1 **teaspoon vanilla**
½ **teaspoon almond extract**
½ **cup toasted wheat germ**
1 **cup dried cranberries and/or golden raisins**

1 Preheat oven to 300°F. Lightly butter a large roasting pan. Add oats, coconut, sunflower seeds, and sesame seeds; spread evenly. Bake 20 minutes, stirring twice.

2 Meanwhile, in a small saucepan combine butter, brown sugar, and honey. Cook, stirring constantly, over medium heat until butter is melted and mixture is combined. Remove from heat. Stir in vanilla and almond extract.

3 Carefully remove roasting pan from oven; place on a wire rack. Increase oven temperature to 350°F. Add wheat germ to the granola then pour warm brown sugar mixture over. Stir granola until it is thoroughly coated with brown sugar mixture. Bake 5 minutes more. Remove pan from oven; place on a wire cooling rack.

4 Stir cranberries into granola. With a spatula, firmly press granola in pan, in an even layer. Bake 20 minutes more or until golden brown, stirring twice. Spread granola on a large piece of foil. Cool completely.

5 Store in an airtight container up to 2 weeks. Makes 8½ cups.

PER SERVING 97 **CAL**; 4 g **FAT** (2 g **SAT**); 4 mg **CHOL**; 23 mg **SODIUM**; 15 g **CARB**; 2 g **FIBER**; 2 g **PRO**

PB&J SMOOTHIES

PB&J Smoothies

Kids will love this smoothie inspired by a favorite sandwich—and with 15 grams of protein per serving, it has real staying power.

MAKES 2 servings **START TO FINISH** 10 minutes

½   **cup plain yogurt**
½   **cup milk**
1   **ripe banana, cut up and frozen**
2   **to 3 tablespoons creamy peanut butter**
2   **tablespoons grape jelly or ¼ cup frozen mixed berries or raspberries**
    Grapes and grape jelly (optional)

1 In a blender combine yogurt, milk, banana, peanut butter, and jelly. Cover and blend until nearly smooth.

2 If desired, top smoothies with grape jelly then gently swirl with a spoon, and serve with grapes on a decorative wooden pick.

PER SERVING 293 **CAL**; 11 g **FAT** (3 g **SAT**); 12 mg **CHOL**; 146 mg **SODIUM**; 38 g **CARB**; 3 g **FIBER**; 15 g **PRO**

Raspberry-Citrus Swirly Smoothies

On a warm summer day, this creamy two-fruit smoothie is a refreshing and light way to start the day.

MAKES 2 servings **START TO FINISH** 15 minutes

½   **cup frozen unsweetened raspberries**
½   **cup orange juice**
2   **6-ounce cartons vanilla yogurt**
1   **ripe banana, peeled, cut up, and frozen**
2   **tablespoons honey**
½   **teaspoon vanilla**

1 In a blender combine raspberries and juice. Cover and blend until smooth. Divide between two glasses.

2 Wash the blender container. In the blender combine yogurt, banana, honey, and vanilla. Cover and blend until smooth. Pour over raspberry mixture in glasses. Swirl with a spoon.

PER SERVING 335 **CAL**; 2 g **FAT** (1 g **SAT**); 10 mg **CHOL**; 87 mg **SODIUM**; 74 g **CARB**; 3 g **FIBER**; 6 g **PRO**

CHAPTER 3

meals in minutes

Get a fresh, delicious dinner on the table in about 30 minutes.

MEXICAN BLACK BEAN
AND CHICKEN PLATTER

BEEF

Asian-Glazed Flank Steak with Blistered Beans, 51

Quick Skillet Steaks with Mushrooms, 50

FISH AND SEAFOOD

Lemon Shrimp with Spinach Quinoa, 66

MEATLESS

Black Bean Cakes with Salsa, 69

Fettuccine with Roasted Cauliflower and Honey-Mustard Sauce, 68

Wild Mushroom Ravioli Skillet Lasagna, 67

PORK

Pork Medallions with Cherry Sauce, 53

Pork Rhubarb Skillet, 54

Quick Mu Shu Pork, 52

Three-Cheese Tortellini in Brown Butter Sauce, 55

POULTRY

Balsamic Chicken and Vegetables, 62

Chicken Marsala, 59

Chicken-Peanut Stir-Fry, 64

Coconut Chicken Noodle Bowl, 56

Mexican Black Bean and Chicken Platter, 60

Pan-Fried Chicken with Polenta and Vegetables, 57

Rotisserie Chicken Banh Mi, 62

White Bean-Turkey Chili with Corn Bread Dumplings, 65

Quick Skillet Steaks with Mushrooms

These restaurant-quality steaks served with red wine sauce are elegant enough for company but can be prepared as a quick weeknight meal as well.

MAKES 4 servings **START TO FINISH** 30 minutes

2	**8-ounce boneless beef top loin steaks, cut ¾ to 1 inch thick**
½	**teaspoon cracked black pepper**
¼	**teaspoon salt**
1	**teaspoon olive oil**
8	**ounces fresh mushrooms, quartered**
1	**cup frozen small whole onions**
4	**cloves garlic, minced**
¾	**cup dry red wine**
1	**cup 50% less sodium beef broth**
2	**tablespoons whole wheat flour**
	Fresh Italian parsley (optional)

1 Trim fat from steaks. Sprinkle steaks with pepper and salt. Heat a large skillet over medium-high heat. Add oil; swirl to lightly coat skillet. Reduce heat to medium. Add steaks; cook 8 to 10 minutes or until medium rare (145°F), turning once. Transfer steaks to a tray or plate; cover with foil and let stand while preparing sauce.

2 For sauce, in the same skillet cook mushrooms and onions over medium-high heat 5 minutes or until tender, stirring frequently. Add garlic; cook and stir 1 minute more. Carefully add wine. Boil gently, uncovered, 5 minutes, stirring occasionally. In a small bowl combine broth and flour; stir into mushroom mixture. Cook and stir until thickened and bubbly; cook and stir 1 minute more.

3 Cut steaks in half and return to skillet; heat through, turning to coat steaks with sauce. Transfer steaks and sauce to dinner plates. If desired, serve with parsley.

PER SERVING 287 **CAL**; 11 g **FAT** (4 g **SAT**); 64 mg **CHOL**; 330 mg **SODIUM**; 11 g **CARB**; 2 g **FIBER**; 28 g **PRO**

Asian-Glazed Flank Steak with Blistered Green Beans

"Blistering" the green beans means they are cooked in very hot oil until they are caramelized and brown in spots. It's a simple way to add terrific flavor to the finished dish.

MAKES 4 servings **START TO FINISH** 35 minutes

1	**pound beef flank steak**
1	**tablespoon cloves minced garlic**
1	**tablespoon finely chopped fresh ginger**
2	**tablespoons soy sauce**
1	**teaspoon packed brown sugar**
2	**to 3 tablespoons peanut oil**
1	**pound green beans, trimmed**
4	**green onions, white parts only, thinly sliced**
2	**tablespoons sweet rice wine (mirin)**
1	**teaspoon red chile paste (sambal oelek)**
	Hot cooked jasmine rice (optional)
	Sesame seeds, toasted (tip, page 8) (optional)

1. Cut flank steak across the grain into thin slices. In a bowl combine garlic and ginger. In another bowl combine soy sauce and brown sugar.

2 In an extra-large skillet or wok heat 2 tablespoons oil over medium-high heat. Add green beans; cook and stir 7 to 8 minutes or until beans are blistered and brown in spots. Transfer beans to paper towels to drain. If necessary, add the remaining 1 tablespoon oil to skillet.

3 Add garlic-ginger to skillet; cook and stir 30 seconds. Add half the beef strips to skillet. Cook and stir 3 minutes or just until beef is browned. Using a slotted spoon, transfer to a bowl. Repeat with the remaining beef. Return all beef to skillet. Stir in green onions, rice wine, chile paste, and the soy sauce-sugar mixture; cook and stir 1 minute. Add green beans; cook 2 minutes or until beans are heated. If desired, serve with hot cooked rice and sprinkle with sesame seeds.

PER SERVING 312 **CAL**; 16 g **FAT** (5 g **SAT**); 53 mg **CHOL**;
672 mg **SODIUM**; 15 g **CARB**; 4 g **FIBER**; 28 g **PRO**

Quick Mu Shu Pork

Preshredded cabbage and carrot (coleslaw mix) and bottled hoisin or plum sauce make this Chinese restaurant favorite doable at home on any day of the week.

MAKES 4 servings   **START TO FINISH** 20 minutes

12	ounces boneless pork top loin chops
1	tablespoon vegetable oil
3	cups sliced fresh button mushrooms (8 ounces)
½	cup bias-sliced green onions
4	cups packaged shredded cabbage with carrot (coleslaw mix)
2	tablespoons soy sauce
1	teaspoon toasted sesame oil
⅛	teaspoon crushed red pepper
8	7- to 8-inch flour tortillas, warmed
¼	cup hoisin sauce or plum sauce

1 Trim fat from meat. Cut meat into thin strips. In a large skillet or wok heat vegetable oil over medium-high heat. Add meat; cook and stir 2 to 3 minutes or until slightly pink in center. Remove from skillet.

2 Add mushrooms and green onions to hot skillet. Cook about 3 minutes or until mushrooms are tender, stirring occasionally. Add cabbage with carrot; cook and stir 1 minute or just until cabbage is wilted.

3 Return meat to skillet. Stir in soy sauce, sesame oil, and crushed red pepper; heat through. Serve with tortillas and hoisin sauce.

PER SERVING 400 **CAL**; 13 g **FAT** (3 g **SAT**); 57 mg **CHOL**; 1,066 mg **SODIUM**; 43 g **CARB**; 4 g **FIBER**; 27 g **PRO**

Pork Medallions with Cherry Sauce

Fresh cherries will have a slightly firmer texture than frozen cherries, but of course pitted frozen cherries are much quicker to prepare.

MAKES 4 servings **START TO FINISH** 25 minutes

1	**pound pork tenderloin**
¼	**teaspoon salt**
¼	**teaspoon black pepper**
	Nonstick cooking spray
¾	**cup cranberry juice, cherry juice, or apple juice**
2	**teaspoons spicy brown mustard**
1	**teaspoon cornstarch**
1	**cup fresh sweet cherries (such as Rainier or Bing), halved and pitted, or 1 cup frozen unsweetened pitted dark sweet cherries, thawed**
	Mashed potatoes (optional)
	Snipped fresh Italian parsley (optional)

1 Cut pork crosswise into 1-inch slices. Place each slice between two pieces of plastic wrap. Using the flat side of a meat mallet, lightly pound each slice into a ½-inch thick medallion. Discard plastic wrap. Sprinkle pork with salt and black pepper.

2 Coat a large unheated nonstick skillet with cooking spray. Heat skillet over medium-high heat. Add pork medallions and cook 6 minutes or until pork is slightly pink in center and juices run clear, turning once. Transfer to a serving platter; cover with foil to keep warm.

3 For cherry sauce, in a small bowl stir together cranberry juice, mustard, and cornstarch; add to skillet. Cook and stir until thickened and bubbly. Cook and stir 2 minutes more. Stir in cherries. Serve cherry sauce with pork. If desired, serve with mashed potatoes and sprinkle with fresh parsley.

PER SERVING 178 **CAL**; 2 g **FAT** (1 g **SAT**); 74 mg **CHOL**; 247 mg **SODIUM**; 13 g **CARB**; 1 g **FIBER**; 24 g **PRO**

Pork Rhubarb Skillet

Pork goes particularly well with fruit of all kinds—cherries, apples, pears, berries, pineapple—and tart rhubarb too.

MAKES 4 servings **START TO FINISH** 30 minutes

1	tablespoon vegetable oil
1	pound lean boneless pork, cut into bite-size strips
1	medium onion, cut into thin wedges
1½	cups sliced fresh rhubarb or frozen unsweetened sliced rhubarb, thawed
1	medium cooking apple, cored and sliced
1	cup chicken broth
2	tablespoons packed brown sugar
1	tablespoon cornstarch
1	tablespoon snipped fresh sage
½	teaspoon salt
¼	teaspoon black pepper
2	cups hot cooked couscous

1 In an extra-large skillet heat oil over medium-high heat. Add pork to skillet. Cook and stir 3 to 4 minutes or until browned. Remove pork from skillet.

2 Add onion to skillet. Cook and stir 2 to 3 minutes or until tender. Add rhubarb and apple; cook 3 to 4 minutes or until crisp-tender.

3 For sauce, in a small bowl combine broth, brown sugar, cornstarch, sage, salt, and pepper. Add to skillet; cook and stir until thickened and bubbly. Add pork to skillet; heat through. Serve over hot cooked couscous.

PER SERVING 342 **CAL**; 11 g **FAT** (3 g **SAT**); 64 mg **CHOL**; 565 mg **SODIUM**; 32 g **CARB**; 3 g **FIBER**; 28 g **PRO**

Three-Cheese Tortellini in Brown Butter Sauce

Brown butter, called "beurre noisette"—literally "hazelnut butter" because it of its color and nutty flavor—is made by gently cooking butter until the solids caramelize and separate from the butterfat.

MAKES 6 servings **START TO FINISH** 30 minutes

1	20-ounce package refrigerated three-cheese tortellini
2	tablespoons olive oil
2	ounces prosciutto, cut into 1-inch pieces, or deli ham
½	cup unsalted butter
1	tablespoon honey (optional)
1	5-ounce package fresh baby spinach
	Salt and black pepper
¼	cup finely shredded Parmigiano-Reggiano cheese (2 ounces)

1 In a large saucepan cook tortellini in salted boiling water with 1 tablespoon of the oil 7 to 9 minutes or until tender; drain. Return tortellini to hot saucepan; cover and keep warm.

2 Meanwhile, in a large skillet heat the remaining oil over medium heat. Add prosciutto; cook until crisp. Remove prosciutto and drain on paper towels. Drain fat from skillet.

3 For brown butter sauce, add butter to the skillet. Cook over medium heat until butter is melted and begins to brown and smell nutty. If desired, stir in honey.

4 Transfer tortellini to a serving bowl. Add spinach and the brown butter sauce; toss gently to coat. Season to taste with salt and pepper. Top with prosciutto and cheese.

PER SERVING 527 **CAL**; 30 g **FAT** (15 g **SAT**); 93 mg **CHOL**; 878 mg **SODIUM**; 46 g **CARB**; 3 g **FIBER**; 20 g **PRO**

Coconut Chicken Noodle Bowl

This Asian-style dish is a wonderful combination of sweet and spicy flavors, soft and crunchy textures, and warm and cool temperatures.

MAKES 6 servings   **START TO FINISH** 30 minutes

8	ounces dry banh pho (Vietnamese wide rice noodles), other wide rice noodles, or 4 cups cooked vermicelli
1	rotisserie chicken
2	limes
½	cup unsweetened coconut milk
2	tablespoons fish sauce or reduced-sodium soy sauce
¼	teaspoon crushed red pepper
⅓	cup finely chopped lightly salted peanuts
¼	cup snipped fresh basil
2	tablespoons canola oil
2	cups fresh snow pea pods, trimmed
1	cup packaged fresh julienned carrots
1	tablespoon finely chopped fresh ginger

1 Place banh pho in a large bowl. Add enough very hot tap water to cover; let stand 10 to 15 minutes or until pliable but not soft. Drain well in a colander. (Skip this step if using cooked vermicelli.)

2 Meanwhile, remove meat from chicken, discarding skin and bones. Coarsely shred chicken; set aside.

3 For sauce, finely shred one lime to yield 1 teaspoon peel and juice both limes to yield 3 tablespoons lime juice*. In a small bowl combine the lime juice, coconut milk, fish sauce, and crushed red pepper; set aside. For topping, in another small bowl combine the peanuts, basil, and lime peel.

4 In a large wok or nonstick skillet heat 1 tablespoon of the oil over medium-high heat. Cook snow peas and carrots 2 minutes, stirring occasionally. Add ginger; cook and stir 30 seconds.

5 Add remaining oil to the wok. Add drained noodles; cook and stir 2 minutes. Add the sauce and chicken. Cook and stir 1 to 2 minutes or until heated through. Sprinkle noodle bowl with peanut topping.

* One lime yields about 2 tablespoons juice.

PER SERVING 430 **CAL**; 18 g **FAT** (5 g **SAT**); 100 mg **CHOL**; 984 mg **SODIUM**; 38 g **CARB**; 2 g **FIBER**; 29 g **PRO**

Pan-Fried Chicken with Polenta and Vegetables

Halving the chicken breasts horizontally creates a thin scallop of meat that cooks very quickly. Dipping them in buttermilk and dredging in seasoned flour before frying gives them a lovely, crisp coating.

MAKES 4 servings **START TO FINISH** 30 minutes

1	**pint grape or cherry tomatoes**
1	**tablespoon packed brown sugar**
3	**cups water**
1	**teaspoon salt**
¾	**cup quick-cooking polenta**
⅓	**cup all-purpose flour**
½	**teaspoon salt**
½	**teaspoon black pepper**
2	**8-ounce skinless, boneless chicken breast halves, halved horizontally**
3	**tablespoons vegetable oil**
¼	**9-ounce package spinach**

1 Pierce tomatoes with a sharp knife. Place in a microwave-safe bowl; sprinkle with brown sugar. Cover loosely. Microwave on high 3 minutes or until skins burst and tomatoes are soft, stirring once; set aside.

2 In a large saucepan bring the water and the 1 teaspoon salt to boiling; stir in polenta. Reduce heat; cook 5 minutes, stirring frequently.

3 In a shallow dish combine flour, the ½ teaspoon salt, and the ½ teaspoon pepper; pour buttermilk into another shallow dish. Dip chicken in buttermilk, then in flour, turning to coat. In an extra-large skillet heat oil over medium-high heat; add chicken. Cook 6 to 8 minutes or until no longer pink (165°F), turning to cook evenly. Remove chicken from skillet.

4 Discard pan drippings. Add spinach to hot skillet; cook and toss just until wilted. Season to taste with additional salt and pepper. Serve chicken with spinach, polenta, and tomatoes.

PER SERVING 506 **CAL**; 14 g **FAT** (2 g **SAT**); 75 mg **CHOL**; 483 mg **SODIUM**; 59 g **CARB**; 8 g **FIBER**; 33 g **PRO**

Chicken Marsala

This classic Italian dish of pan-fried chicken and mushrooms draped in a sauce flavored with Marsala—a wine fortified with brandy—is wonderful with either cooked pasta or rice.

MAKES 4 servings **START TO FINISH** 35 minutes

- ¼ **cup all-purpose flour**
- ½ **teaspoon dried thyme, crushed**
- ¼ **teaspoon salt**
- ⅛ **teaspoon black pepper**
- 4 **6- to 8-ounce skinless, boneless chicken breast halves**
- 1 **cup chicken broth**
- ½ **cup dry Marsala**
- 3 **tablespoons butter**
- 1 **tablespoon olive oil**
- 2 **cups sliced fresh button or cremini mushrooms**
- 2 **tablespoons finely chopped shallot**
- **Hot cooked pasta (optional)**
- **Fresh thyme (optional)**

1 In a shallow dish stir together flour, thyme, salt, and pepper; set aside. Place each chicken breast half between two pieces of plastic wrap. Using the flat side of a meat mallet, pound chicken lightly to about ¼-inch thickness. Remove plastic wrap. Dip chicken pieces into flour mixture, turning to coat both sides.

2 In a small bowl whisk together any remaining flour mixture, the broth, and Marsala; set aside.

3 In an extra-large skillet heat 1 tablespoon of the butter and the oil over medium-high heat. Add chicken; cook 4 to 6 minutes or until no longer pink, turning once. Transfer chicken to a serving platter; cover and keep warm.

4 For sauce, add mushrooms and shallot to skillet; cook 6 to 8 minutes or until tender, stirring occasionally. Carefully add Marsala mixture. Cook and stir until slightly thickened and bubbly. Whisk in the remaining butter until incorporated.

5 Spoon sauce over chicken and, if desired, pasta. Sprinkle with thyme, if desired.

PER SERVING 381 **CAL**; 17 g **FAT** (7 g **SAT**); 133 mg **CHOL**; 638 mg **SODIUM**; 11 g **CARB**; 1 g **FIBER**; 39 g **PRO**

Mexican Black Bean and Chicken Platter

You will have more canned chipotle chile peppers in adobo sauce than you need. Divide the remaining chiles into 1- or 2-chile portions and freeze in small plastic bags.

MAKES 6 servings **START TO FINISH** 30 minutes

¼   **cup cider vinegar**

3   **tablespoons olive oil or vegetable oil**

3   **tablespoons snipped fresh cilantro**

1   **canned chipotle chile pepper in adobo sauce, drained and finely chopped (tip, page 11)**

1   **clove garlic, minced**

½   **teaspoon salt**

1   **15-ounce can black beans, rinsed and drained**

¾   **cup cooked fresh or frozen whole kernel corn**

½   **cup chopped orange or yellow sweet pepper (optional)**

10 **grape tomatoes, halved**

¼   **cup sliced green onions**

3½ **cups shredded cooked chicken**

10 **cups coarsely shredded lettuce**

1   **avocado, halved, seeded, peeled, and sliced (optional)**

1   **lime halved and cut into wedges**

1 For dressing, in a screw-top jar combine vinegar, oil, cilantro, chipotle pepper, garlic, and salt. Cover; shake well.

2 In a bowl combine black beans, corn, and, if desired, sweet pepper. Drizzle with 2 tablespoons dressing; toss gently to coat. Stir in tomatoes and green onions.

3 Line a large serving platter with shredded lettuce. Arrange chicken on lettuce. Spoon black bean mixture on chicken. Drizzle remaining dressing. Serve with avocados, if desired, and lime wedges.

PER SERVING 319 **CAL**; 14 g **FAT** (3 g **SAT**); 73 mg **CHOL**; 533 mg **SODIUM**; 22 g **CARB**; 6 g **FIBER**; 30 g **PRO**

Balsamic Chicken and Vegetables

A blend of vegetables—asparagus, carrot, and tomato—lends color and healthfulness to this very light and low-calorie dish.

MAKES 4 servings **START TO FINISH** 30 minutes

¼	cup bottled Italian salad dressing
2	tablespoons balsamic vinegar
1	tablespoon honey
⅛	to ¼ teaspoon crushed red pepper
2	tablespoons olive oil
1	pound chicken breast tenderloins
10	ounces fresh asparagus, trimmed and cut into 2-inch pieces
1	cup purchased shredded carrot
⅓	cup chopped, seeded tomato

1 For the sauce, in a small bowl stir together salad dressing, vinegar, honey, and crushed red pepper. Set aside.

2 In a large skillet heat oil over medium-high heat. Add chicken; cook 5 to 6 minutes or until chicken is tender and no longer pink (170°F), turning once. Add half the sauce to skillet; turn chicken to coat. Transfer chicken to a serving platter; cover and keep warm.

3 Add asparagus and carrot to skillet. Cook and stir 3 to 4 minutes or until asparagus is crisp-tender; transfer to serving platter.

4 Stir remaining sauce; add to skillet. Cook and stir 1 minute, scraping up browned bits from bottom of skillet. Drizzle sauce over chicken and vegetables. Sprinkle with tomato.

PER SERVING 269 **CAL**; 12 g **FAT** (2 g **SAT**); 66 mg **CHOL**; 323 mg **SODIUM**; 12 g **CARB**; 2 g **FIBER**; 27 g **PRO**

Rotisserie Chicken Banh Mi

You can use any kind of leftover roasted or grilled meat—pork, turkey, chicken, or beef—in this Vietnamese-style sandwich.

MAKES 4 servings **START TO FINISH** 30 minutes

⅓	cup white vinegar
¼	cup sugar
⅛	teaspoon salt
1	cup shredded carrots
¼	cup light mayonnaise or salad dressing
1	to 2 teaspoons Asian chili sauce (sriracha sauce)
½	teaspoon reduced-sodium soy sauce
⅛	teaspoon sugar
1	8-ounce French bread baguette, halved lengthwise
8	ounces shredded rotisserie chicken breast meat
⅓	long seedless cucumber, cut into thin spears (about 3 ounces)
1	fresh jalapeño, thinly sliced (tip, page 11) (optional)
⅓	cup fresh cilantro leaves

1 Preheat oven to 425°F. In a small bowl combine vinegar, the ¼ cup sugar, and the salt; stir until sugar is dissolved. Add carrots; toss well. Let stand 15 minutes.

2 Meanwhile, in another small bowl combine mayonnaise, Asian chili sauce, soy sauce, and the ⅛ teaspoon sugar.

3 Place baguette halves, cut sides up, on rack in oven; bake 5 minutes or just until warm and lightly crisped. Spread chili mayonnaise on cut sides of baguette. Place chicken on baguette halves. Drain carrots, pressing to drain off excess liquid; arrange on chicken. Top with cucumber and, if desired, jalapeño. Sprinkle with cilantro leaves. Cut into four portions.

PER SERVING 358 **CAL**; 8 g **FAT** (2 g **SAT**); 49 mg **CHOL**; 840 mg **SODIUM**; 51 g **CARB**; 2 g **FIBER**; 21 g **PRO**

ROTISSERIE CHICKEN
BANH MI

Chicken-Peanut Stir-Fry

Cook the frozen stir-fry vegetables of your choice very briefly—just 2 to 3 minutes—to retain their color, crisp texture, and nutrition.

MAKES 4 servings **START TO FINISH** 25 minutes

1	**14-ounce can unsweetened light coconut milk**
⅓	**cup peanut butter**
½	**teaspoon salt**
½	**teaspoon ground ginger**
¼	**teaspoon crushed red pepper**
1	**pound skinless, boneless chicken breast halves, cut into 1-inch pieces**
	Salt and black pepper
1	**tablespoon canola oil or vegetable oil**
2	**cups frozen desired stir-fry vegetables**
½	**cup frozen peas**
4	**cups hot cooked brown or white rice**

1 For sauce, in a medium bowl whisk together coconut milk, peanut butter, salt, ginger, and crushed red pepper. Set aside.

2 Lightly season chicken with salt and black pepper. In a large skillet or wok heat oil over medium-high heat. Add chicken; cook 6 minutes or until no longer pink, turning to brown evenly. Remove from skillet.

3 Add stir-fry vegetables and peas to hot skillet. Cook and stir 2 to 3 minutes or until heated through.

4 Add sauce to skillet; return chicken to skillet. Gently stir all ingredients together to coat with sauce; heat through. Serve chicken over hot cooked rice.

PER SERVING 754 **CAL**; 37 g **FAT** (15 g **SAT**); 73 mg **CHOL**; 836 mg **SODIUM**; 64 g **CARB**; 5 g **FIBER**; 42 g **PRO**

White Bean-Turkey Chili with Corn Bread Dumplings

This warming bowl of chili is a great way to use leftover cooked turkey. A package of corn bread mix makes quick work of the tender dumplings.

MAKES 4 servings **START TO FINISH** 25 minutes

- 1 **pound cooked turkey, chopped**
- 1 **16-ounce jar chunky salsa**
- 1 **15-ounce can cannellini beans (white kidney beans), rinsed and drained**
- 1 **teaspoon chili powder**
- ⅔ **cup water**
- 1 **8½-ounce package corn bread mix**
- 1 **egg**
- ¼ **cup water**
  Black pepper
- ¼ **cup shredded cheddar cheese (optional)**
  Slivered green onions (optional)

1 In Dutch oven combine turkey, salsa, beans, and chili powder. Stir in the ⅔ cup water. Bring to boiling.

2 Meanwhile, for dumplings, in a medium bowl mix together corn bread mix, egg, and the ¼ cup water. Drop batter by large spoonfuls onto boiling chili. Reduce heat.

3 Cover and simmer 10 to 15 minutes or until a wooden pick inserted into a dumpling comes out clean. Season to taste with pepper. If desired, sprinkle with cheese and green onions.

PER SERVING 555 **CAL**; 15 g **FAT** (4 g **SAT**); 140 mg **CHOL**; 1,618 mg **SODIUM**; 64 g **CARB**; 11 g **FIBER**; 47 g **PRO**

Lemon Shrimp with Spinach Quinoa

Quinoa has a natural coating of a substance called saponin, which can make it taste bitter or soapy. Rinsing it before cooking removes it. Most boxed or packaged quinoa is prerinsed, but it doesn't hurt to rinse it again.

MAKES 4 servings **START TO FINISH** 30 minutes

1	**pound fresh or frozen large shrimp in shells**
1	**recipe Spinach Quinoa**
1	**teaspoon all-purpose flour**
⅓	**cup dry white wine or ¼ cup reduced-sodium chicken broth plus 1 tablespoon white wine vinegar**
2	**tablespoons lemon juice**
⅛	**teaspoon ground black pepper**
1	**tablespoon unsalted butter**
½	**cup thinly sliced red onion**
	Lemon wedges (optional)

1 Thaw shrimp, if frozen. Prepare Spinach Quinoa. Meanwhile, peel and devein shrimp, leaving tails intact, if desired. Rinse shrimp; pat dry with paper towels. Place shrimp in a large bowl. Sprinkle with flour; toss to coat.

2 For sauce, in a small bowl stir together wine, lemon juice, and pepper.

3 In a large skillet melt butter over medium-high heat. Add onion; cook about 5 minutes or until tender, stirring occasionally. Add shrimp to skillet. Cook and stir 1 to 2 minutes or until shrimp start to turn opaque. Carefully add sauce to skillet; bring to boiling. Cook and stir about 1 minute or until shrimp are opaque and sauce is thickened.

4 To serve, spoon shrimp mixture over Spinach Quinoa. If desired, serve with lemon wedges.

Spinach Quinoa Rinse and drain ½ cup red quinoa or regular quinoa. In a small saucepan bring 1 cup water to boiling. Stir in quinoa; 1 clove garlic, minced; and ¼ teaspoon salt. Return to boiling; reduce heat. Simmer, covered, about 15 minutes or until liquid is absorbed. Stir in 2 cups packaged fresh baby spinach and ½ teaspoon finely shredded lemon peel.

PER SERVING 227 **CAL**; 6 g **FAT** (2 g **SAT**); 137 mg **CHOL**; 287 mg **SODIUM**; 19 g **CARB**; 2 g **FIBER**; 21 g **PRO**

Wild Mushroom Ravioli Skillet Lasagna

This saucy pasta dish has all of the ingredients and great flavors of traditional layered lasagna—tomato sauce, toothsome pasta, and multiple types of cheese—but is ready to eat in minutes instead of hours.

MAKES 4 servings **START TO FINISH** 25 minutes

1	egg, lightly beaten
½	15-ounce carton fat-free ricotta cheese
2	tablespoons grated Romano or Parmesan cheese
2	cups lower sodium pasta sauce with basil
¾	cup water
2	8- to 9-ounce packages refrigerated wild mushroom-filled ravioli or agnolotti
2	cups chopped fresh kale
	Grated Romano or Parmesan cheese (optional)

1 In a medium bowl combine egg, ricotta cheese, and the 2 tablespoons Romano cheese; set aside.

2 In a large skillet combine pasta sauce and the water. Bring to boiling. Stir in ravioli and kale. Return to boiling; reduce heat. Spoon ricotta mixture into large mounds on top of ravioli mixture.

3 Simmer, covered, 10 minutes or until ricotta mixture is set and ravioli is tender but still firm. If desired, sprinkle with additional Romano cheese.

PER SERVING 416 **CAL**; 16 g **FAT** (7 g **SAT**); 118 mg **CHOL**; 975 mg **SODIUM**; 45 g **CARB**; 4 g **FIBER**; 26 g **PRO**

Fettuccine with Roasted Cauliflower and Honey-Mustard Sauce

Roasting has a magical effect on cauliflower—giving it a deliciously crispy and browned exterior and a buttery, tender interior.

MAKES 4 servings   **START TO FINISH** 30 minutes

6	cups sliced or chopped cauliflower florets
1	tablespoon olive oil
⅛	teaspoon black pepper
4	ounces dried whole grain fettuccine
1	cup packaged fresh julienned carrots
½	cup thinly sliced green onions
2	tablespoons coarse-ground mustard
2	tablespoons honey
½	teaspoon salt
¼	cup snipped fresh cilantro
¼	cup chopped unsalted peanuts

1 Preheat oven to 450°F. Place cauliflower in a shallow baking pan. Drizzle with oil and sprinkle with pepper; toss to coat. Roast, uncovered 15 to 20 minutes or just until cauliflower is tender and lightly browned, stirring twice.

2 Meanwhile, cook fettuccine according to package directions, adding carrots the last 2 minutes of cooking. Before draining, remove ¼ cup pasta cooking water; set aside. Drain pasta and carrots; transfer to a large bowl. Add roasted cauliflower and green onions; toss to combine.

3 For the sauce, in a small bowl combine the reserved pasta cooking water, mustard, honey, and salt. Add sauce to pasta and vegetables; toss to coat. Sprinkle servings with cilantro and peanuts.

PER SERVING 270 **CAL**; 9 g **FAT** (1 g **SAT**); 0 mg **CHOL**; 458 mg **SODIUM**; 42 g **CARB**; 8 g **FIBER**; 9 g **PRO**

Black Bean Cakes with Salsa

Leave off the sour cream and these crisp vegetarian black bean cakes are suitable fare for vegans as well.

MAKES 4 servings **START TO FINISH** 25 minutes

1½	**cups purchased salsa**
2	**15-ounce cans black beans, rinsed and drained**
1	**8.5-ounce package corn muffin mix**
1	**medium fresh jalapeño, seeded and finely chopped (tip, page 11)**
2½	**teaspoons chili powder**
2	**tablespoons olive oil**
½	**cup sour cream**
½	**teaspoon chili powder**

1 Drain ½ cup of the salsa in a colander. In a large bowl mash drained beans with a potato masher or fork. Stir in drained salsa, muffin mix, half of the jalapeño, and the 2½ teaspoons chili powder.

2 In an extra-large skillet heat 1 tablespoon of the oil over medium-high heat. Drop four ½-cup mounds of the bean mixture into hot oil. Using a spatula, flatten mounds into 3½-inch cakes. Cook 6 minutes or until brown, turning once. Remove from skillet. Repeat with the remaining oil and bean mixture.

3 In a small bowl combine sour cream and the ½ teaspoon chili powder. Top bean cakes with the remaining salsa, the remaining jalapeño chile pepper, and seasoned sour cream.

PER SERVING 519 **CAL**; 19 g **FAT** (4 g **SAT**); 11 mg **CHOL**; 1,553 mg **SODIUM**; 79 g **CARB**; 12 g **FIBER**; 20 g **PRO**

cook it slowly

Come home to the aroma of something wonderful bubbling in the slow cooker.

EGG ROLL-STYLE BOWL

BEEF

Beef Chili Mac, 73

Chipotle-Black Bean Chili, 74

German-Style Beef Roast, 72

Meatball Hoagies, 75

CHICKEN AND TURKEY

Chicken and Veggie Burritos, 86

Chicken Cacciatore, 84

Chicken Goulash with Peas and Caraway, 82

General Tso's Chicken and Noodles, 85

Indian Chicken Stew, 83

Primavera Chicken Vegetable Soup, 86

MEATLESS

Low-Country Shrimp Boil, 89

Summer Vegetable Curry, 89

PORK

Brat and Sauerkraut Soup, 81

Egg Roll-Style Bowl, 79

Five-Spice Ribs with Crunchy Cabbage Slaw, 81

Peppery Pulled Pork Sandwiches with Tangy Barbecue Sauce, 76

Spicy Carnitas with Cherry-Peach Salsa, 78

German-Style Beef Roast

Use a whole-grain or coarse-grain mustard in this hearty pot roast dish. The tiny seeds add both piquant flavor and texture to the cooking liquid.

MAKES 8 servings **PREP** 25 minutes **SLOW COOK** 8 hours (low) or 4 hours (high)

- 1 **2½- to 3-pound boneless beef chuck pot roast**
- 1 **tablespoon cooking oil**
- 2 **cups sliced carrots**
- 2 **cups chopped onion**
- 1 **cup sliced celery**
- ¾ **cup chopped kosher-style dill pickle**
- ½ **cup dry red wine or beef broth**
- ⅓ **cup German-style mustard**
- ½ **teaspoon coarse ground black pepper**
- ¼ **teaspoon ground cloves**
- 2 **bay leaves**
- 2 **tablespoons all-purpose flour**
- 2 **tablespoons dry red wine or beef broth**
  Hot cooked noodles or cooked spaetzle
  Snipped fresh parsley (optional)

1 Trim fat from meat. If necessary, cut roast to fit into a 3½- or 4-quart slow cooker. In a large skillet brown the meat on all sides in hot oil. Drain off fat.

2 In the slow cooker combine the carrots, onion, celery, and pickle. Place the meat on top of vegetables. In a small bowl combine the ½ cup red wine, the mustard, pepper, cloves, and bay leaves. Pour over meat and vegetables in cooker.

3 Cover and cook on low 8 to 10 hours or on high 4 to 5 hours. Using a slotted spoon, remove meat and vegetables from cooker and place on a serving platter; cover with foil to keep warm.

4 For gravy, transfer cooking liquid to a 2-quart saucepan; skim off fat and discard bay leaves. In a small bowl stir together flour and the 2 tablespoons wine. Stir into the cooking liquid. Cook and stir over medium heat until thickened and bubbly, then cook 1 minute more. Serve meat, vegetables, and gravy with noodles. If desired, sprinkle with parsley.

PER SERVING 256 **CAL**; 7 g **FAT** (2 g **SAT**); 84 mg **CHOL**; 467 mg **SODIUM**; 10 g **CARB**; 2 g **FIBER**; 31 g **PRO**

Beef Chili Mac

Use the corn or tortilla chips to scoop up the saucy meat, beans, and noodles.

MAKES 6 servings   **PREP** 25 minutes   **SLOW COOK** 4 hours (low) or 2 hours (high)

1½   **pounds ground beef**
1   **cup chopped onion**
3   **cloves garlic, minced**
1   **15-ounce can chili beans in chili gravy**
1   **14.5-ounce can diced tomatoes and green chiles, undrained**
1   **cup beef broth**
¾   **cup chopped green sweet pepper**
2   **teaspoons chili powder**
1   **teaspoon ground cumin**
¼   **teaspoon salt**
8   **ounces dried cavatappi or macaroni**
   Corn chips or tortilla chips
   Shredded cheddar cheese (optional)

1 In a large skillet cook ground beef, onion, and garlic over medium heat until meat is browned and onion is tender. Drain off fat.

2 Place meat, undrained chili beans, undrained tomatoes and green chiles, broth, sweet pepper, chili powder, cumin, and salt in a 3½- or 4-quart slow cooker.

3 Cover and cook on low 4 to 6 hours or on high 2 to 3 hours.

4 Cook pasta according to package directions; drain well. Stir in chili. Serve with corn chips. If desired, top with cheese.

PER SERVING 559 **CAL**; 22 g **FAT** (7 g **SAT**); 77 mg **CHOL**; 871 mg **SODIUM**; 57 g **CARB**; 8 g **FIBER**; 33 g **PRO**

Chipotle-Black Bean Chili

Hominy is dried corn that has had the hull and germ removed—and which is then rehydrated. The texture is delightfully chewy. It can be served as a side dish or stirred into soups and stews.

MAKES 6 servings   **PREP** 20 minutes   **SLOW COOK** 7 hours (low) and 3½ hours (low)

1½	**pounds ground beef, ground pork, or ground turkey**
2	**14-ounce cans reduced-sodium beef broth or chicken broth**
1	**16-ounce jar chunky salsa**
1	**15-ounce can black beans, rinsed and drained**
1	**15-ounce can golden hominy, rinsed and drained**
2	**cups loose-pack frozen diced hashbrown potatoes with onions and peppers**
1	**to 2 canned chipotle chile peppers in adobo sauce, finely chopped (tip, page 11)**
2	**teaspoons chili powder**
1	**teaspoon dried oregano, crushed**
1	**teaspoon ground cumin**
	Sour cream, chopped avocado, and/or shredded cheddar cheese (optional)
	Tortilla chips or corn bread (optional)

1 In a large skillet cook ground beef until meat is browned. Drain off fat. Transfer meat to a 4- to 5-quart slow cooker. Stir in broth, salsa, beans, hominy, hashbrowns, chipotle peppers, chili powder, oregano, and cumin.

2 Cover and cook on low 7 to 8 hours or on high 3½ to 4 hours.

3 If desired, top with sour cream, avocado, and/or cheddar cheese, and serve with tortilla chips.

PER SERVING 450 **CAL**; 24 g **FAT** (9 g **SAT**); 81 mg **CHOL**; 1,287 mg **SODIUM**; 34 g **CARB**; 8 g **FIBER**; 27 g **PRO**

Meatball Hoagies

These wonderfully sloppy and delicious sandwiches make perfect party food for football-watching with friends.

MAKES 8 servings   **PREP** 30 minutes   **BAKE** 25 minutes   **SLOW COOK** 3 hours (low) or 1½ hours (high)

- 1   egg, lightly beaten
- ⅓   cup fine dry bread crumbs
- ⅔   cup finely chopped onion
- ½   teaspoon salt
- ½   teaspoon dried oregano, crushed
- ½   teaspoon black pepper
- 1½   pounds lean ground beef
- 1   15-ounce can tomato sauce
- ½   cup chopped green sweet pepper
- 2   tablespoons packed brown sugar
- 1   tablespoon yellow mustard
- 1   teaspoon chili powder
- ¼   teaspoon garlic salt
- ⅛   teaspoon bottled hot pepper sauce
- 8   hoagie buns, split and toasted
- 2   cups shredded mozzarella cheese (8 ounces)

1 Preheat oven to 350°F. In a large bowl stir together egg, bread crumbs, half the onion, the salt, oregano, and ¼ teaspoon of the black pepper. Add ground beef; mix well. Shape into 32 balls. Arrange meatballs in a single layer in an ungreased 15×10×1-inch baking pan. Bake, uncovered, 25 minutes. Drain off fat.

2 For the sauce, in a 3½- or 4-quart slow cooker stir together tomato sauce, the remaining onion, the sweet pepper, brown sugar, mustard, chili powder, garlic salt, the remaining black pepper, and the hot pepper sauce. Add cooked meatballs, stirring gently to coat with sauce.

3 Cover and cook on low 3 to 4 hours or on high 1½ to 2 hours.

4 Place four meatballs in each bun. Top with sauce and cheese.

PER SERVING 724 **CAL**; 28 g **FAT** (11 g **SAT**); 99 mg **CHOL**; 1,504 mg **SODIUM**; 84 g **CARB**; 5 g **FIBER**; 36 g **PRO**

Peppery Pulled Pork Sandwiches with Tangy Barbecue Sauce

When you have a hungry crowd coming over and little time to cook, get the fixings for these saucy sandwiches going in the slow cooker—and then go about your day.

MAKES 12 servings **PREP** 25 minutes **COOK** 10 hours (low) or 5 hours (high) + 15 minutes (high)

1	**2½- to 3-pound boneless pork blade Boston roast (or Boston butt roast)**
4	**teaspoons Spanish bittersweet smoked paprika, smoked paprika, or hot paprika**
1½	**teaspoons freshly ground black pepper**
½	**teaspoon salt**
2	**tablespoons vegetable oil**
2	**medium onions, cut into thin wedges**
1	**14.5-ounce can diced tomatoes with chili spices, undrained**
1¾	**cups apple juice**
6	**cloves garlic, minced**
½	**cup ketchup**
½	**cup cider vinegar**
¼	**cup Worcestershire sauce**
12	**soft white hamburger buns, toasted**

1 Trim fat from meat. If necessary, cut meat to fit a 4- to 5-quart slow cooker. Sprinkle meat with 2 teaspoons of the smoked paprika, 1 teaspoon of the black pepper, and the salt; rub in with your fingers. In a large skillet brown meat on all sides in hot oil over medium heat. Drain off fat. Transfer meat to cooker. Add onions, undrained tomatoes, apple juice, and garlic to slow cooker.

2 Cover and cook on low 10 to 11 hours or on high 5 to 5½ hours.

3 Meanwhile, for barbecue sauce, in a small saucepan combine ketchup, vinegar, Worcestershire sauce, remaining smoked paprika, and remaining black pepper. Bring to boiling; reduce heat. Simmer, uncovered, 15 minutes, stirring occasionally. Remove from heat.

4 Transfer meat to cutting board, reserving cooking liquid in slow cooker. Shred meat with two forks.

5 Pour cooking liquid into a 4-cup measure; skim off fat. Return meat to slow cooker; stir in barbecue sauce and enough cooking liquid to reach desired consistency. Cover and cook on high 15 minutes or until heated through. Serve on toasted buns.

PER SERVING 370 **CAL**; 16 g **FAT** (5 g **SAT**); 59 mg **CHOL**; 655 mg **SODIUM**; 34 g **CARB**; 2 g **FIBER**; 22 g **PRO**

Spicy Carnitas with Cherry-Peach Salsa

If you like your carnitas with a kick, use the larger number of chipotle chiles in adobo sauce—and even a little more sauce, if you like.

MAKES 10 servings **PREP** 25 minutes **SLOW COOK** 8 hours (low) or 4 hours (high)

1	4-pound boneless pork shoulder roast
½	teaspoon salt
¼	teaspoon black pepper
1	tablespoon vegetable oil
1	12-ounce can cherry-flavor cola
½	cup bottled barbecue sauce
½	cup chopped onion
2	to 4 canned chipotle peppers in adobo sauce, minced, plus 2 tablespoons adobo sauce (tip, page 11)
2	cloves garlic, minced
5	cups hot cooked rice
1	recipe Cherry-Peach Salsa
	Warmed corn or flour tortillas (optional)

1 Trim fat from meat. Cut meat into 2-inch pieces. Sprinkle meat with salt and pepper; toss gently to coat.

2 In a large skillet heat oil over medium-high heat. Cook meat, one-third at a time, in hot oil until browned. Using a slotted spoon, transfer meat to a 4- to 5-quart slow cooker. Add cola, barbecue sauce, onion, chipotle peppers and adobo sauce, and garlic. Stir to combine.

3 Cover and cook on low 8 to 10 hours or on high 4 to 5 hours. Using a slotted spoon, transfer meat to serving plates. Serve with rice, Cherry-Peach Salsa, and, if desired, warmed tortillas.

Cherry-Peach Salsa In a medium bowl combine 1½ cups pitted, halved dark sweet cherries; 1½ cups coarsely chopped, peeled peaches; ⅓ cup chopped fresh cilantro; 2 tablespoons lime juice; 1 tablespoon honey; 2 teaspoons minced, seeded jalapeño (tip, page 11); and ¼ teaspoon salt.

PER SERVING 459 **CAL**; 13 g **FAT** (4 g **SAT**); 108 mg **CHOL**; 752 mg **SODIUM**; 46 g **CARB**; 2 g **FIBER**; 37 g **PRO**

Egg Roll-Style Bowl

This recipe features the flavors of those favorite Asian deep-fried appetizers—but in a healthful and warming soup.

MAKES 8 servings **PREP** 30 minutes **SLOW COOK** 6 hours (low) or 3 hours (high)

6	cups packaged shredded cabbage with carrot (coleslaw mix)
1¼	pounds lean ground pork, broken up
1	cup chopped bok choy or fresh spinach leaves
1	cup chopped red sweet pepper
½	cup finely chopped sweet onion
½	cup finely chopped celery
¼	cup finely chopped green onions
¼	cup soy sauce
3	tablespoons tomato paste
2	tablespoons red miso paste
2	tablespoons sake or cream sherry
1	tablespoon rice vinegar
1	teaspoon dried thyme, crushed
½	teaspoon salt
¼	teaspoon black pepper
4	cups reduced-sodium chicken broth

1 In a 3½- or 4-quart slow cooker combine all the ingredients.

2 Cover and cook on low 6 hours or on high 3 hours.

PER SERVING 247 **CAL**; 15 g **FAT** (6 g **SAT**); 51 mg **CHOL**; 1,215 mg **SODIUM**; 10 g **CARB**; 2 g **FIBER**; 16 g **PRO**

FIVE-SPICE RIBS WITH
CRUNCHY CABBAGE SLAW

Five-Spice Ribs with Crunchy Cabbage Slaw

Five-spice powder is an aromatic blend of star anise, cloves, cinnamon, Szechuan pepper, and fennel that is widely used in Chinese cooking.

MAKES 6 servings **PREP** 40 minutes
SLOW COOK 7 hours (low) or 3½ hours (high)

3	pounds boneless pork country-style ribs
1½	teaspoons Chinese five-spice powder
⅓	cup water
⅓	cup reduced-sodium soy sauce
1	tablespoon honey
½	teaspoon crushed red pepper
6	⅛-inch slices fresh unpeeled ginger
3	cloves garlic, unpeeled and smashed
1	recipe Crunchy Cabbage Slaw

1 Trim fat from ribs; sprinkle with Chinese five-spice powder. Place in a 4- to 5-quart slow cooker.

2 In a small bowl stir together the water, the soy sauce, honey, and crushed red pepper. Pour over meat in cooker. Add ginger and garlic. Cover and cook on low 7 to 8 hours or on high 3½ to 4 hours.

3 Using a slotted spoon, transfer ribs to a serving platter; cover to keep warm. Skim fat from cooking liquid. Strain cooking liquid; discard solids. Serve cooking liquid and Crunchy Cabbage Slaw alongside ribs.

Crunchy Cabbage Slaw In a large bowl combine 3 cups shredded green cabbage, 3 cups shredded red cabbage, ¾ cup thin red sweet pepper strips, and ¾ cup thin strips yellow sweet pepper. For dressing, in a screw-top jar combine ¼ cup canola oil, 3 tablespoons cider vinegar, 2 tablespoons pure maple syrup, 1 teaspoon celery seeds, ½ teaspoon salt, and ¼ teaspoon freshly ground black pepper. Cover and shake well. Pour dressing over slaw; toss to coat.

PER SERVING 570 **CAL**; 34 g **FAT** (6 g **SAT**); 166 mg **CHOL**; 817 mg **SODIUM**; 16 g **CARB**; 2 g **FIBER**; 46 g **PRO**

Brat and Sauerkraut Soup

Serve this warming soup with crusty multigrain or pumpernickel rolls.

MAKES 6 servings **PREP** 30 minutes
SLOW COOK 6 hours (high) or 3 hours (low)

1	pound uncooked bratwurst, cut into ½-inch slices
1	pound tiny new red potatoes, cut into quarters
2	small onions, cut into ¼-inch wedges or coarsely chopped
1	cup sliced celery
2	cloves garlic, minced
3	bay leaves
1	14.5-ounce can Bavarian-style sauerkraut
2	14.5-ounce cans lower-sodium beef broth
1	tablespoon spicy brown mustard
1	tablespoon cider vinegar
1	teaspoon paprika
1	teaspoon fennel seeds, crushed
½	teaspoon caraway seeds
	Sour cream (optional)

1 In a large skillet cook bratwurst slices over medium-high heat 3 to 4 minutes or until browned on all sides, stirring frequently. Remove from skillet and set aside.

2 In a 4- to 5-quart slow cooker combine potatoes, onions, celery, garlic, and bay leaves. Top with browned bratwurst and sauerkraut. In a large bowl whisk together broth, mustard, vinegar, paprika, fennel seeds, and caraway seeds. Pour into cooker.

3 Cover and cook on low 6 to 7 hours or on high 3 to 3½ hours. Discard bay leaves. If desired, top each serving with sour cream.

PER SERVING 355 **CAL**; 20 g **FAT** (7 g **SAT**); 55 mg **CHOL**; 1,335 mg **SODIUM**; 27 g **CARB**; 2 g **FIBER**; 17 g **PRO**

Chicken Goulash with Peas and Caraway

If you can't find ground chicken, ground turkey—all breast or a blend of white and dark meat—works just fine in this dish.

MAKES 8 servings **PREP** 20 minutes **SLOW COOK** 5 hours (low) or 2½ hours (high) **STAND** 10 minutes

1	tablespoon olive oil
1½	pounds ground chicken
1	medium onion, quartered and thinly sliced
1½	cups chopped red sweet peppers
1	8-ounce can no-salt-added tomato sauce
1	cup reduced-sodium chicken broth
½	cup sauerkraut, rinsed and drained
2	tablespoons sweet paprika
2	tablespoons tomato paste
4	cloves garlic, minced
1	teaspoon caraway seeds, crushed
½	teaspoon dried marjoram, crushed
¼	teaspoon black pepper
3	cups dried elbow macaroni
1	cup frozen peas

1 In a large skillet heat oil over medium heat. Add ground chicken and onion; cook until chicken is browned.

3 In a 3½- or 4-quart slow cooker combine cooked chicken and onion, sweet peppers, tomato sauce, broth, sauerkraut, paprika, tomato paste, garlic, caraway seeds, marjoram, and black pepper.

2 Cover and cook on low 5 to 6 hours or on high 2½ to 3 hours.

4 Shortly before serving, cook macaroni according to package directions; drain. Stir cooked macaroni and frozen peas into cooker. Let stand, covered, 10 minutes before serving.

PER SERVING 346 **CAL**; 10 g **FAT** (2 g **SAT**); 73 mg **CHOL**; 284 mg **SODIUM**; 42 g **CARB**; 5 g **FIBER**; 23 g **PRO**

Indian Chicken Stew

For an authentic touch, serve this stew over aromatic and nutty-tasting basmati rice, the traditional Indian rice.

MAKES 8 servings **PREP** 15 minutes **SLOW COOK** 8 hours (low) or 4 hours (high)

Nonstick cooking spray

2 pounds skinless, boneless chicken thighs, cut into 1-inch pieces

½ cup onion, chopped

3 cloves garlic, minced

5 teaspoons curry powder

2 teaspoons ground ginger

½ teaspoon salt

¼ teaspoon black pepper and/or cayenne pepper

2 15-ounce cans garbanzo beans (chickpeas), rinsed and drained

2 14.5-ounce cans diced tomatoes, undrained

1 cup chicken broth

1 bay leaf

2 tablespoons lime juice

1 9-ounce package fresh spinach (optional)

4 cups hot cooked rice (optional)

1 Line a 6-quart slow cooker with a disposable slow cooker liner. Lightly coat liner with cooking spray. Add chicken, onion, garlic, curry powder, ginger, salt, and pepper; toss to coat. Stir in beans, tomatoes, broth, and bay leaf.

2 Cover and cook on low 8 to 10 hours or on high 4 to 5 hours.

3 Stir lime juice into stew. If desired, stir in spinach; let stand 2 to 3 minutes or until spinach begins to wilt. If desired, serve with hot cooked rice.

PER SERVING 295 **CAL**; 6 g **FAT** (1 g **SAT**); 94 mg **CHOL**; 867 mg **SODIUM**; 32 g **CARB**; 7 g **FIBER**; 29 g **PRO**

Chicken Cacciatore

Fresh herbs are best stirred into a dish at the end of cooking—as is done in this traditional Italian dish—while dried herbs are best added at the beginning of cooking.

MAKES 6 servings **PREP** 25 minutes **COOK** 6 hours (low) or 3 hours (high)

⅓ **cup all-purpose flour**
3½ **to 4 pounds meaty chicken pieces (breast halves, thighs, and drumsticks), skinned**
2 **tablespoons olive oil**
2 **cups thinly sliced fresh cremini and/or button mushrooms**
1 **14.5-ounce can diced tomatoes, drained**
1¼ **cups chopped green sweet pepper**
1 **cup chopped onion**
1 **cup chopped carrots**
½ **cup dry white wine**
½ **teaspoon salt**
½ **teaspoon black pepper**
2 **tablespoons snipped fresh basil**
2 **tablespoons snipped fresh Italian parsley**
1 **teaspoon fresh thyme leaves**

1 Place flour in a plastic bag. Add chicken pieces, a few at a time, shaking to coat. In an extra-large nonstick skillet, heat oil over medium-high heat. Cook chicken, half at a time if necessary, in hot oil for 12 minutes or until browned, turning occasionally. Transfer to a 5- to 6-quart slow cooker.

2 Add mushrooms to skillet; cook and stir over medium-high heat 3 minutes. Transfer mushrooms to cooker. Add drained tomatoes, sweet pepper, onion, carrots, wine, salt, and pepper to cooker.

3 Cover and cook on low 6 to 7 hours or on high 3 to 3½ hours. Before serving, stir in basil, parsley, and thyme.

PER SERVING 310 **CAL**; 8 g **FAT** (2 g **SAT**); 110 mg **CHOL**; 445 mg **SODIUM**; 16 g **CARB**; 3 g **FIBER**; 38 g **PRO**

General Tso's Chicken and Noodles

A generous shot of sriracha sauce gives this Chinese-style dish some serious heat. If you like your food less spicy, cut the amount in half, to just 1 tablespoon. You can also vary the heat level with the type of chile you use (see tip, below).

MAKES 6 servings **PREP** 25 minutes **LOW COOK** 4 hours (low) or 2 hours (high)

- 1½ **pounds skinless, boneless chicken breast halves, cut into 1-inch pieces**
- ½ **cup chicken broth**
- 2 **tablespoons sriracha sauce**
- 2 **tablespoons soy sauce**
- 2 **tablespoons rice vinegar**
- 1 **tablespoon honey**
- 1 **tablespoon ketchup**
- 4 **cloves garlic, minced**
- 1 **teaspoon quick-cooking tapioca, crushed**
- 4 **dried red chiles***
- 12 **ounces dried egg noodles, cooked**
- 1 **tablespoon rice wine or dry sherry**
- ⅓ **cup chopped green onions**
- ⅓ **cup chopped peanuts**

1 Place chicken pieces in a 3½- or 4-quart slow cooker. In a bowl whisk together broth, sriracha sauce, soy sauce, vinegar, honey, ketchup, garlic, and tapioca; pour over chicken. Add dried chiles.

2 Cover and cook on low 4 to 5 hours or on high 2 to 2½ hours.

3 Remove and discard chiles. Just before serving, stir in cooked noodles and rice wine. Sprinkle servings with green onions and chopped peanuts.

*Choose from Anaheim for mild heat, Guajillo for medium heat, or chipotle for hot and smoky heat.

PER SERVING 439 **CAL**; 10 g **FAT** (2 g **SAT**); 131 mg **CHOL**; 618 mg **SODIUM**; 49 g **CARB**; 3 g **FIBER**; 37 g **PRO**

Primavera Chicken Vegetable Soup

"Primavera" means spring in Italian. It also refers to dishes featuring lots of vegetables, particularly those in season in spring—such as the carrots, asparagus, and peas in this light and lovely soup.

MAKES 4 servings **PREP** 15 minutes
SLOW COOK 7 hours (low) or 3½ hours (high)
+ 30 minutes (high)

2	whole chicken legs (drumstick and thigh), skinned (1¼ pounds total)
1	32-ounce carton chicken broth
1	cup coarsely chopped carrots
½	cup sliced celery
½	cup dry white wine or chicken broth
½	teaspoon dried thyme, crushed
½	teaspoon ground sage
¼	teaspoon dried rosemary, crushed
¼	teaspoon black pepper
3	cloves garlic, minced
1	cup asparagus spears cut into 1-inch pieces (8 ounces)
½	cup frozen peas
¼	cup sliced green onions
	Coarsely snipped fresh Italian parsley (optional)

1 Place chicken in a 3½- or 4-quart slow cooker. Add broth, carrots, celery, wine, thyme, sage, rosemary, black pepper, and garlic.

2 Cover and cook on low 7 to 8 hours or on high 3½ to 4 hours.

3 Transfer chicken to a platter. If using low-heat setting, turn to high. When chicken is cool enough to handle, remove meat from bones; discard bones. Using two forks, pull chicken apart into shreds and return to cooker. Stir in asparagus, peas, and green onions.

4 Cover and cook 30 minutes more or until heated through. If desired, sprinkle with parsley.

PER SERVING 250 **CAL**; 6 g **FAT** (1 g **SAT**); 113 mg **CHOL**; 1,105 mg **SODIUM**; 11 g **CARB**; 3 g **FIBER**; 33 g **PRO**

Chicken and Veggie Burritos

The zucchini is added just 35 minutes before the end of cooking time so that it retains its crisp-tender texture.

MAKES 8 servings **PREP** 25 minutes
SLOW COOK 6 hours (low) or 2½ hours (high)
+ 30 minutes (high) **STAND** 5 minutes

1	large green sweet pepper, cubed
1	cup coarsely chopped onion
1	cup coarsely chopped celery
1½	pounds skinless, boneless chicken breast halves, cut into ½-inch-wide strips
1	8-ounce bottle green taco sauce
1	teaspoon instant chicken bouillon granules
½	teaspoon ground cumin
2	medium zucchini, cut in half lengthwise
½	cup uncooked instant rice
8	9- to 10-inch spinach, chile, or plain flour tortillas, warmed*
1	cup chopped tomatoes
¾	cup shredded Monterey Jack cheese with jalapeño peppers (3 ounces)
¼	cup sliced green onions

1 In a 3½- or 4-quart slow cooker combine sweet pepper, onion, and celery. Add chicken. In a bowl combine taco sauce, bouillon granules, and cumin. Pour over chicken.

2 Cover and cook on low 6 to 7 hours or high 2½ to 3 hours. Cut zucchini into ½-inch slices. Stir into cooker. Cover and cook 30 minutes more. Stir in uncooked rice. Cover and let stand 5 minutes.

3 Divide chicken and veggie filling among warmed tortillas. Top with tomatoes, cheese, and green onions. Fold tortilla over filling; fold in opposite sides and roll up.

*Tip To warm tortillas, preheat oven to 350°F. Stack tortillas and wrap tightly in foil. Place in oven for 10 minutes or until heated through.

PER SERVING 328 **CAL**; 8 g **FAT** (3 g **SAT**); 59 mg **CHOL**; 603 mg **SODIUM**; 35 g **CARB**; 3 g **FIBER**; 27 g **PRO**

CHICKEN AND VEGGIE BURRITOS

LOW-COUNTRY
SHRIMP BOIL

Low-Country Shrimp Boil

Cooking this Louisiana classic in a slow cooker means you don't have to stand by the stove and watch the pot. For a very casual and convivial gathering serve the shrimp, sausage, and vegetables on parchment paper in the center of the table.

MAKES 6 servings **PREP** 15 minutes
SLOW COOK 7 hours (low) or 3½ hours (high)
+ 10 minutes (high)

4	cups reduced-sodium chicken broth or water
1	pound tiny red or yellow new potatoes
14	to 16 ounces cooked andouille or kielbasa sausage, cut into 1½-inch pieces
½	cup frozen small whole onions, thawed
½	to 1 tablespoon Old Bay seasoning or crab and shrimp boil seasoning
¼	to ½ teaspoon cayenne pepper
3	ears fresh sweet corn, husks and silks removed, and cut crosswise into quarters
1½	pounds fresh or frozen large shrimp in shells, thawed
2	tablespoons butter, melted
1	tablespoon snipped fresh Italian parsley Cocktail sauce

1 In a 6- to 7-quart slow cooker combine the broth, potatoes, sausage, onions, Old Bay seasoning, and cayenne pepper. Place corn on potato mixture. Cover and cook on low 7 to 8 hours or on high 3½ to 4 hours or just until corn and potatoes are tender.

2 If using low, turn to high. Gently stir shrimp into the cooker. Cover and cook 10 minutes or until shrimp are opaque.

3 Using a slotted spoon, transfer shrimp, potatoes, sausage, onions, and corn to an extra-large bowl; drizzle with butter and some of the cooking liquid. Sprinkle with parsley and serve with cocktail sauce.

PER SERVING 416 **CAL**; 16 g **FAT** (6 g **SAT**); 193 mg **CHOL**; 1,583 mg **SODIUM**; 31 g **CARB**; 3 g **FIBER**; 39 g **PRO**

Summer Vegetable Curry

Make this sweet and savory curry with vegetable broth which is suitable to serve to vegans.

MAKES 6 servings **PREP** 25 minutes
SLOW COOK 5 hours (low) or 2½ hours (high)

3	cups cauliflower florets
1	15- to 16-ounce can garbanzo beans (chickpeas), rinsed and drained
8	ounces green beans, cut into 1-inch pieces (1¾ cups)
8	ounces new potatoes, coarsely chopped
1	cup sliced carrots
½	cup chopped onion
⅓	cup golden raisins (optional)
1	14.5-ounce can chicken broth or vegetable broth
3	to 4 teaspoons curry powder
¼	teaspoon salt
¼	teaspoon crushed red pepper
1	14-ounce can unsweetened coconut milk
3	cups hot cooked rice
¼	cup shredded fresh basil leaves
¼	cup chopped dry roasted peanuts (optional)

1 In a 4- to 5-quart slow cooker combine cauliflower, garbanzo beans, green beans, potatoes, carrots, onion, and, if desired, raisins. Stir in broth, curry powder, salt, and crushed red pepper.

2 Cover and cook on low 5 to 6 hours or on high 2½ to 3 hours.

3 Stir coconut milk into cooker. Serve vegetable curry over rice. Top with basil and, if desired, peanuts.

PER SERVING 323 **CAL**; 11 g **FAT** (9 g **SAT**); 1 mg **CHOL**; 488 mg **SODIUM**; 47 g **CARB**; 7 g **FIBER**; 9 g **PRO**

CHAPTER 5

great grilling

Fire up for the flavor smoke and fire give to your favorite foods.

GRILLED WATERMELON-SHRIMP SALAD

BEEF

The Heart and Seoul of Korea Burgers, 99

Indian-Spiced Burgers with Cilantro
Cucumber Sauce, 96

Strip Steaks Adobado, 95

Stuffed Bacon and Cheese Curd Burger, 100

Sweet and Spicy Steak Salad, 95

CHICKEN

Chicken Salad with Creamy
Tarragon-Shallot Dressing, 102

Lemon-Herb Grilled Chicken, 101

FISH AND SEAFOOD

Grilled Dijon Salmon, 103

Grilled Stuffed Green Chiles, 105

Grilled Watermelon-Shrimp Salad, 106

Southwestern Stuffed Roasted Peppers, 105

PORK

Sticky Mocha Caramelized Ribs, 92

Sticky Mocha Caramelized Ribs

A rub made with coffee, cocoa, and spices was the jumping off point for Sherry Ricci's prizewinning ribs in the 2014 Gnarly Head Rib Challenge. The finishing touch on these ribs is a glaze made with red wine, sugar, unsweetened chocolate, and whipping cream. When the Mendon, New York, cook isn't working part-time as a dental hygienist, she's in the kitchen or traveling to cooking contests. These tasty ribs fetched her a $5,000 cash prize.

MAKES 6 servings **PREP** 25 minutes **CHILL** 2 hours **GRILL** 1 hour 40 minutes

2	**tablespoons instant coffee crystals or finely ground coffee**
1	**tablespoon smoked paprika**
1	**tablespoon unsweetened cocoa powder**
2	**teaspoons sea salt**
2	**teaspoons black pepper**
1	**teaspoon sweet paprika**
½	**teaspoon cayenne pepper**
6	**pounds pork loin baby back ribs**
¼	**cup sugar**
¼	**cup Gnarly Head Old Vine Zinfandel**
¼	**cup water**
¾	**cup whipping cream**
4	**ounces finely chopped unsweetened chocolate**
¼	**teaspoon sea salt**
	Sea salt flakes

1 For rub, in a bowl combine coffee, smoked paprika, cocoa powder, 2 teaspoons sea salt, black pepper, sweet paprika, and cayenne pepper. Sprinkle rub over both sides of ribs; rub in with your fingers. Cover ribs with plastic wrap; refrigerate at least 2 hours or up to overnight.

2 Grease the grill rack. Prepare grill for indirect heat using a drip pan. Place ribs, bone sides down, over drip pan. Grill, covered, 1½ hours. (Do not turn ribs while grilling).

3 Meanwhile, for the glaze, in a heavy saucepan stir together sugar, wine, and the water over medium heat until sugar is dissolved. Turn heat to high; cover and boil 2 minutes. Uncover and continue to boil until glaze is lightly thickened. Stir until glaze is the consistency of maple syrup. Remove from heat and stir in whipping cream. Add chocolate; stir until melted. Stir in ¼ teaspoon sea salt.

4 Brush both sides of ribs with the glaze*. Return ribs to grill over direct heat. Grill 10 to 15 minutes more, without turning. Before serving, sprinkle ribs with sea salt flakes.

*Refrigerate leftover glaze in an airtight storage container up to 1 week.

PER SERVING 823 **CAL**; 59 g **FAT** (26 g **SAT**); 235 mg **CHOL**; 1,134 mg **SODIUM**; 16 g **CARB**; 3 g **FIBER**; 57 g **PRO**

STRIP STEAKS ADOBADO

Strip Steaks Adobado

Strip steaks—also called beef top loin steaks—have a slender strip of fat along one edge that gets crisp, browned, and smoky on the grill.

MAKES 6 servings **PREP** 25 minutes **MARINATE** 4 hours
GRILL 10 minutes

3	boneless beef top loin steaks, cut 1 inch thick (2½ to 3 pounds total)
¼	cup red wine vinegar
¼	cup olive oil
1	tablespoon ground ancho or pasilla chile pepper
3	cloves garlic, minced
1	teaspoon packed brown sugar
1	teaspoon dried oregano, crushed
1	teaspoon ground coriander
½	teaspoon salt
¼	teaspoon ground allspice
	Salt

1 Trim fat from steaks. Place steaks in a resealable plastic bag set in a shallow dish. For marinade, in a small bowl combine vinegar, oil, ground ancho pepper, garlic, brown sugar, oregano, coriander, ½ teaspoon salt, and allspice. Pour marinade over steaks. Seal bag; turn to coat steaks. Marinate in the refrigerator 4 to 8 hours, turning bag occasionally.

2 Drain steaks, discarding marinade. Sprinkle steaks with additional salt.

3 Grill steaks, covered, over medium heat 10 to 12 minutes for medium rare (145°F) or 12 to 15 minutes for medium (160°F), turning once.

PER SERVING 327 **CAL**; 18 g **FAT** (5 g **SAT**); 127 mg **CHOL**; 360 mg **SODIUM**; 2 g **CARB**; 1 g **FIBER**; 41 g **PRO**

Sweet and Spicy Steak Salad

Freezing the meat for about 30 minutes before preparing it allows you to slice it thinly and more neatly.

MAKES 4 servings **PREP** 30 minutes **MARINATE** 6 hours
GRILL 8 minutes

1	pound boneless beef top sirloin steak, cut ¾ inch thick
¾	cup bottled raspberry vinaigrette
¼	cup raspberry spreadable fruit jam
2	tablespoons snipped fresh cilantro
1	chipotle chile pepper in adobo sauce, drained and finely chopped (tip, page 11)
1	4-ounce package semisoft goat cheese (chèvre)
6	cups baby arugula or baby spinach
4	roma or small tomatoes, cut into wedges
1	avocado, sliced
2	cups sliced fresh mushrooms
	Snipped chives and cracked black pepper (optional)

1 If desired, partially freeze beef (about 30 minutes) for easy slicing. Trim fat from meat. Thinly slice meat across the grain into strips. Place meat in a resealable plastic bag.

2 For dressing, in a small bowl whisk together the vinaigrette, jam, cilantro, and chipotle pepper. Pour ½ cup dressing over beef and turn to coat. Marinate in the refrigerator 6 hours or overnight, turning occasionally. Chill remaining dressing, covered, until ready to serve.

3 Meanwhile, shape the goat cheese into 12 balls. Chill, covered, on a small plate until ready to use.

4 Drain the meat; discard marinade. Thread meat in accordion fashion onto bamboo skewers*, leaving ¼ inch between pieces. Grill meat, covered, over medium heat, 8 to 12 minutes or until desired doneness, turning once.

5 Spread arugula on a platter. Arrange cheese balls, tomato wedges, avocado, and mushrooms on arugula. Place meat kabobs on mushrooms. If desired, top with chives and pepper. Whisk the remaining dressing; drizzle over salad or pass separately.

*Soak bamboo skewers in water to cover 30 minutes before threading meat.

PER SERVING 489 **CAL**; 24 g **FAT** (9 g **SAT**); 112 mg **CHOL**; 390 mg **SODIUM**; 28 g **CARB**; 4 g **FIBER**; 44 g **PRO**

Indian-Spiced Burgers with Cilantro Cucumber Sauce

The yogurt sauce served with these highly spiced burgers is essentially raita, a cucumber-yogurt sauce traditionally served with Indian curries to help cool the fire.

MAKES 4 servings **PREP** 25 minutes **GRILL** 14 minutes

1	**5.3- to 6-ounce container fat-free plain Greek yogurt**
⅔	**cup finely chopped cucumber**
¼	**cup snipped fresh cilantro**
2	**cloves garlic, minced**
⅛	**teaspoon salt**
⅛	**teaspoon black pepper**
½	**cup canned garbanzo beans (chickpeas), rinsed and drained**
1	**pound lean ground beef**
¼	**cup finely chopped red onion**
2	**tablespoons finely chopped jalapeño, seeded, if desired (tip, page 11)**
½	**teaspoon salt**
¼	**teaspoon ground cumin**
¼	**teaspoon ground coriander**
⅛	**teaspoon cinnamon**
⅛	**teaspoon black pepper**
	Cracked black pepper (optional)
4	**radicchio leaves, shredded**
	Grilled Naan or other flatbread (optional)

1 For sauce, in a small bowl stir together yogurt, cucumber, cilantro, garlic, and ⅛ teaspoon each salt and black pepper. Cover and chill until ready to serve.

2 In a medium bowl using a potato masher or fork, mash garbanzo beans. Add the beef, onion, jalapeño, the ½ teaspoon salt, cumin, coriander, cinnamon, and ⅛ teaspoon black pepper; mix well. Form into four ¾-inch thick patties.

3 Grill patties, covered, over medium heat for 14 to 18 minutes or until done (160°F), turning once.

4 Top patties with sauce and sprinkle with cracked black pepper, if desired. Serve with shredded radicchio and, if desired, grilled Naan.

PER SERVING 258 **CAL**; 12 g **FAT** (5 g **SAT**); 75 mg **CHOL**; 539 mg **SODIUM**; 8 g **CARB**; 2 g **FIBER**; 29 g **PRO**

The Heart and Seoul of Korea Burgers

In 1990, Sutter Home uncorked the wine industry's first big cooking competition—the Build a Better Burger Recipe Contest. Since then, more than 10,000 Sutter Home fans have submitted recipes for wildly imaginative burgers in an effort, says a Sutter Home spokesperson, to demystify the challenge of pairing wine with one of America's favorite foods. This Asian-inspired work of art took top prize—$25,000—at the 2015 contest. And yes, it has Spam in it.

MAKES 6 servings **PREP** 15 minutes **COOK** 5 minutes **GRILL** 14 minutes

2	cups shredded napa cabbage
½	cup honey roasted peanuts, chopped
¼	cup chopped Thai basil
¼	cup minced bottled roasted red sweet pepper
3	tablespoons rice vinegar
1	teaspoon soy sauce
¼	teaspoon toasted sesame oil
1	cup mayonnaise
⅓	cup gochujang*
2	cloves garlic, minced
8	ounces Spam, cut into 1-inch long thin matchsticks
¼	cup minced green onions
1	tablespoon soy sauce
1	teaspoon kosher salt
1	teaspoon toasted sesame oil
½	teaspoon freshly ground black pepper
½	teaspoon finely minced fresh ginger
1	clove garlic, finely minced
2	pounds ground beef (75% to 80% lean) Vegetable oil
6	King's Hawaiian Original Hamburger Buns
6	leaves redleaf lettuce
1½	cups chopped plain rice cakes (roughly 1-inch pieces)

1 For peanut basil slaw, in a large bowl combine cabbage, peanuts, basil, roasted red pepper, rice vinegar, soy sauce, and sesame oil. Toss to combine. Cover and chill until ready to serve. Drain before serving.

2 For mayo, in a small bowl whisk together mayonnaise, gochujang, and garlic. Cover and chill until ready to serve.

3 For crispy spam, heat a large skillet over medium-high heat. Add Spam and cook 5 to 8 minutes or until crispy, stirring occasionally. Transfer to paper towels to drain.

4 For patties, in a large bowl combine green onions, soy sauce, salt, sesame oil, pepper, ginger, and garlic. Add ground beef and combine, handling meat as little as possible to avoid compacting. Divide into six equal portions then form into ¾-inch thick patties.

5 Grease the grill rack. Grill patties, covered, over medium heat 14 to 18 minutes or until done (160°F), turning once. The last few minutes of grilling, place buns, cut sides down, on perimeter of rack to lightly toast.

6 For each burger, spread some of the gochujang mayo on cut sides of each bun, top with a lettuce leaf, some of the crispy Spam, a few pieces of rice cake, a patty, some of the peanut basil slaw, and bun tops.

*Gochujang is a thick Korean hot pepper paste made from chile peppers, glutinous rice, fermented soybeans, and salt. The flavor is garlicky, spicy, fermented, sweet, and salty.

PER SERVING 819 **CAL**; 59 g **FAT** (19 g **SAT**); 153 mg **CHOL**; 1,171 mg **SODIUM**; 33 g **CARB**; 2 g **FIBER**; 36 g **PRO**

Stuffed Bacon and Cheese Curd Burger

Although bacon and cheddar is a classic combination, any flavor of squeaky cheese curds gets meltingly delicious in this fun burger. Try jalapeño, Ranch, Cajun, taco, or garlic and herb—or whatever else suits your fancy.

MAKES 4 servings **PREP** 20 minutes **BAKE** 10 minutes **CHILL** 1 hour **GRILL** 20 minutes

- **4** **thick bacon slices**
- **¼** **cup packed brown sugar**
- **2** **pounds 85%-lean ground chuck or 90%-lean ground sirloin**
- **¾** **cup cheese curds or string cheese, chopped Salt and black pepper**
- **4** **hamburger buns Sliced tomato, white onion, and/or lettuce leaves (optional)**

1 Preheat oven to 450°F. Place bacon slices on the unheated rack of a broiler pan. Sprinkle each slice with brown sugar. Bake 10 minutes or until crisp. When cool enough to handle, chop bacon; set aside.

2 Divide and pat beef into eight patties approximately 4 inches in diameter and about ¾ inch thick.

3 Place one-fourth of the chopped bacon and 3 tablespoons of the cheese curds in the middle of four patties, leaving ½ inch around the edge of patty. Top each with the remaining four patties. Pinch edges of patties together to seal. Refrigerate, covered, at least 1 hour. Season patties with salt and black pepper.

4 Oil the grill rack. Grill patties, covered, over medium heat 20 minutes, or until done (160°F) , turning once, Toast buns, cut sides down, on grill the last 1 to 2 minutes of grilling.

5 Place patties on buns and, if desired, top with tomato, onion, and/or lettuce.

PER SERVING 743 **CAL**; 41 g **FAT** (15 g **SAT**); 166 mg **CHOL**; 686 mg **SODIUM**; 35 g **CARB**; 1 g **FIBER**; 55 g **PRO**

Lemon-Herb Grilled Chicken

For extra lemony flavor, squeeze the grilled lemon halves over the chicken after it comes off the grill. They make an eye-catching garnish as well.

MAKES 8 servings **PREP** 25 minutes **MARINATE** 4 hours **GRILL** 50 minutes

5	to 6 pounds meaty chicken pieces (breast halves, drumsticks, and thighs)
	Kosher salt or regular salt
	Black pepper
¾	cup chicken broth
¼	cup snipped fresh Italian parsley
1	tablespoon lemon zest
⅓	cup lemon juice
3	tablespoons olive oil
1	tablespoon snipped fresh sage or 1 teaspoon dried sage, crushed
1	tablespoon snipped fresh thyme or 1 teaspoon dried thyme, crushed
1	teaspoon crushed red pepper
3	cloves garlic, minced
¼	cup honey
	Lemon halves (optional)

1 Skin chicken pieces, if desired. Sprinkle both sides of chicken with salt and black pepper. Place chicken in a resealable plastic bag or covered dish and set aside.

2 For marinade, in a small bowl combine broth, parsley, lemon zest and juice, oil, sage, thyme, red pepper, and garlic. Pour marinade over chicken and turn to coat. Marinate in the refrigerator 4 to 24 hours, turning occasionally. Remove chicken pieces, reserving marinade. Set chicken aside.

3 Strain marinade through a fine-mesh sieve into a medium saucepan; add honey. Bring to boiling; reduce heat and simmer, uncovered, 15 to 20 minutes or until reduced to a glaze consistency (should have ¼ cup).

4 Prepare grill for indirect heat. Place chicken pieces, bone sides down, on grill rack over drip pan. Grill, covered, over indirect medium heat 50 to 60 minutes or until chicken is tender and no longer pink (170° for breasts; 175° for drumsticks and thighs). Brush with glaze the last 15 minutes of grilling.

5 If desired, place a few lemon halves, cut sides down, on grill the last few minutes of grilling. Serve chicken with grilled lemon halves.

PER SERVING 522 **CAL**; 37 g **FAT** (9 g **SAT**); 144 mg **CHOL**; 61 mg **SODIUM**; 10 g **CARB**; 36 g **PRO**

Chicken Salad with Creamy Tarragon-Shallot Dressing

Licoricey-tasting tarragon is a classic flavor pairing with chicken. If the anise flavor is a bit strong for your palate, use fresh basil instead.

MAKES 4 servings **PREP** 20 minutes **GRILL** 12 minutes **COOK** 13 minutes

4	skinless, boneless chicken thighs (about 12 ounces total)
⅛	teaspoon salt
⅛	teaspoon black pepper
8	ounces fresh green beans, trimmed
	Nonstick cooking spray
1½	cups sliced fresh mushrooms
6	cups torn Bibb lettuce
4	hard-cooked eggs, peeled and sliced
¾	cup grape or cherry tomatoes, halved (optional)
1	recipe Creamy Tarragon-Shallot Dressing

1 Trim fat from chicken. Sprinkle chicken with salt and pepper. Grill chicken thighs, uncovered, directly over medium heat 12 to 15 minutes or until no longer pink (175°F), turning once. Slice chicken into strips. Set aside.

2 Meanwhile, in a medium saucepan cook beans, covered, in enough boiling water to cover 8 to 10 minutes or until tender. Drain and rinse with cold water to cool quickly; drain again and set aside.

3 Coat a large unheated nonstick skillet with cooking spray; heat over medium heat. Cook mushrooms in hot skillet 5 to 7 minutes or until tender and lightly browned, stirring occasionally. Remove from heat and cool slightly.

4 To serve, divide torn lettuce among four serving plates. Top with green beans, cooked mushrooms, sliced eggs, and, if desired, tomatoes. Arrange grilled chicken strips on salads. Drizzle with Creamy Tarragon-Shallot Dressing.

Creamy Tarragon-Shallot Dressing In a small bowl whisk together ⅓ cup buttermilk and 2 tablespoons light mayonnaise. Stir in ¼ cup finely chopped shallots, 1 tablespoon snipped fresh tarragon, ⅛ teaspoon salt, and dash black pepper.

PER SERVING 259 **CAL**; 12 g **FAT** (3 g **SAT**); 287 mg **CHOL**; 359 mg **SODIUM**; 11 g **CARB**; 3 g **FIBER**; 27 g **PRO**

Grilled Dijon Salmon

Serve this healthful grilled salmon with a blend of slender sautéed green beans and halved grape tomatoes.

MAKES 6 servings   **PREP** 15 minutes   **MARINATE** 2 hours   **GRILL** 4 minutes per ½-inch thickness

6	4- to 6-ounce fresh or frozen skinless salmon fillets
¼	cup olive oil
1	teaspoon finely shredded lemon peel
2	tablespoons lemon juice
2	tablespoons dry vermouth, dry white wine, or water
2	teaspoons Dijon mustard
2	teaspoons snipped fresh thyme
2	teaspoons snipped fresh tarragon
2	cloves garlic, minced
½	teaspoon salt
¼	teaspoon cracked black pepper

1 Thaw salmon, if frozen. Rinse salmon; pat dry with paper towels. Place salmon in a resealable plastic bag set in a shallow dish.

2 For marinade, in a small bowl combine oil, lemon peel, lemon juice, vermouth, mustard, thyme, tarragon, garlic, salt, and pepper. Pour marinade over salmon. Seal bag; turn to coat salmon. Marinate in the refrigerator 2 to 4 hours, turning bag once.

3 Drain salmon, discarding marinade. Measure thickness of salmon. Oil the grill rack. Grill salmon, covered, over medium heat 4 to 6 minutes per ½-inch thickness or until fish begins to flake when tested with a fork, turning once.

PER SERVING 250 **CAL**; 16 g **FAT** (2 g **SAT**); 62 mg **CHOL**; 285 mg **SODIUM**; 1 g **CARB**; 23 g **PRO**

GRILLED STUFFED
GREEN CHILES

Grilled Stuffed Green Chiles

These cheese-filled chiles are similar to chiles rellenos—but they're grilled instead of fried.

MAKES 4 servings   **PREP** 30 minutes   **GRILL** 13 minutes
STAND 20 minutes   **CHILL** 1 hour

- 2   cups coarsely chopped tomatoes
- ¼   cup finely chopped sweet onion
- 1   to 2 small fresh serrano or jalapeño peppers, seeded and finely chopped (tip, page 11)
- 1   teaspoon sugar
- ½   teaspoon salt
- 4   large fresh Anaheim chile peppers (tip, page 11)
- 3   ounces soft goat cheese (chèvre) or cream cheese, softened
- 1   cup shredded Colby cheese or Colby and Monterey Jack cheese (4 ounces)
       Dash cayenne pepper
       Vegetable oil

1 For salsa, in a medium bowl combine tomatoes, onion, serrano pepper, sugar, and salt. Cover and chill 1 hour or up to 24 hours.

2 Rinse Anaheim peppers; pat dry. Carefully cut a lengthwise slit along each pepper. Using a small, sharp knife, gently scrape out as much seeds and membrane as possible without tearing peppers. Leave stems attached.

3 Grill peppers, covered, over medium-high heat 10 to 12 minutes or until skin darkens and blisters, turning often.

4 Wrap peppers in foil; let stand 20 minutes. When cool enough to handle, hold peppers under cold running water and carefully peel away blackened skin. Be careful not to tear peppers.

5 In a bowl stir together goat cheese, Colby cheese, and cayenne pepper. Spoon 2 to 3 tablespoons stuffing into each pepper. Do not overstuff. Pinch edges together with cheese to seal. Lightly brush stuffed peppers with oil. If desired, place peppers in a grill basket.

6 Grill stuffed peppers, covered, over medium-high heat 3 to 4 minutes or just until cheese is melted (or grill peppers in basket). Do not turn. Serve warm with salsa.

PER SERVING 278 **CAL**; 21 g **FAT** (10 g **SAT**); 36 mg **CHOL**; 550 mg **SODIUM**; 12 g **CARB**; 2 g **FIBER**; 13 g **PRO**

Southwestern Stuffed Roasted Peppers

The filling for this twist on stuffed peppers includes corn, shrimp, corn bread stuffing, and diced green chiles. The peppers are finished off with a drizzle of Alfredo sauce.

MAKES 4 servings   **PREP** 35 minutes   **GRILL** 18 minutes

- 4   large red, yellow, and/or orange sweet peppers
- 1   tablespoon olive oil
- ½   cup chopped onion
- ½   cup frozen whole kernel corn
- 8   ounces fresh peeled and deveined shrimp, chopped; skinless, boneless chicken breasts, cut into bite-size pieces; and/or bulk pork sausage
- 2   cups corn bread stuffing mix
- 1   cup chicken broth
- 1   4-ounce can diced green chile peppers, undrained
- 1   10-ounce container refrigerated Alfredo pasta sauce
- 1   tablespoon snipped fresh cilantro

1 Grill whole sweet peppers, covered, over medium-high heat 13 to 15 minutes or until charred and very tender, turning occasionally. Wrap peppers in foil. Let stand 15 minutes or until cool enough to handle.

2 Meanwhile, for stuffing, in a large skillet heat oil over medium heat. Add onion, corn, and shrimp, chicken, and/or sausage. Cook until shrimp is opaque, chicken is no longer pink, and/or sausage is browned, stirring occasionally. Stir in stuffing mix and broth; cook just until broth is absorbed. Remove from heat. Stir in half the chile peppers.

3 Using a sharp knife, loosen edges of skins from grilled sweet peppers; gently peel off and discard skins. Brush peppers with oil. Cut each pepper in half lengthwise; remove seeds. Spoon stuffing into pepper halves. Grill 5 minutes or until heated through.

4 For sauce, in a small saucepan combine Alfredo sauce and the remaining green chile peppers. Cook over medium heat until heated through. Spoon sauce over stuffed peppers. Sprinkle with cilantro.

PER SERVING 420 **CAL**; 19 g **FAT** (9 g **SAT**); 121 mg **CHOL**; 1,134 mg **SODIUM**; 44 g **CARB**; 5 g **FIBER**; 20 g **PRO**

Grilled Watermelon-Shrimp Salad

Grilling watermelon caramelizes its natural sugars, heightening its sweetness and giving it attractive grill marks.

MAKES 4 servings   **PREP** 30 minutes   **GRILL** 8 minutes

1	pound fresh or frozen large shrimp in shells
6	tablespoons olive oil
½	teaspoon kosher salt or salt
¼	cup lemon juice
2	tablespoons honey
1	teaspoon crushed red pepper
1	1½-inch slice seedless watermelon, quartered
1	5- to 6-ounce package torn mixed salad greens
½	cup crumbled Gorgonzola cheese or other blue cheese (2 ounces)

1 Thaw shrimp, if frozen. Peel and devein shrimp, leaving tails intact (if desired). Rinse shrimp; pat dry with paper towels. Thread shrimp onto four 10- to 12-inch metal or wooden* skewers, leaving ¼ inch between pieces. Brush shrimp with 2 tablespoons of the oil and sprinkle with ¼ teaspoon of the salt.

2 For vinaigrette, in a small bowl whisk together the remaining oil and salt, lemon juice, honey, and crushed red pepper. Brush watermelon with some of the vinaigrette.

3 Grill shrimp and watermelon, covered, over medium heat. Grill shrimp 4 to 6 minutes or until opaque, and watermelon 8 to 10 minutes or until warm and grill marks are visible, turning once.

4 Divide salad greens among four dinner plates. Top with shrimp and a wedge of watermelon. Whisk remaining vinaigrette; drizzle over salads. Sprinkle with cheese.

*Soak wooden skewers in water 30 minutes before threading shrimp.

PER SERVING 473 **CAL**; 27 g **FAT** (6 g **SAT**); 183 mg **CHOL**; 616 mg **SODIUM**; 33 g **CARB**; 2 g **FIBER**; 28 g **PRO**

CHAPTER 6

healthy favorites

Here's some inspiration to eat right with these delicious, low-calorie dishes.

ROASTED POBLANO CHICKEN WILD RICE

Spicy Skillet Pork Chops

Canned diced tomatoes with green chile gives this Mexican-inspired dish a jump-start on flavor.

MAKES 8 servings **PREP** 20 minutes **COOK** 17 minutes

3	cups frozen whole kernel corn
2	10-ounce cans diced tomatoes and green chiles, undrained
4	cloves garlic, minced
1	teaspoon ground cumin
½	teaspoon bottled hot pepper sauce
8	boneless pork loin chops, cut ¾ inch thick
1	teaspoon chili powder
1	tablespoon vegetable oil
2	medium onions, cut into thin wedges
	Fresh cilantro (optional)
	Hot cooked rice

1 In a medium bowl combine corn, tomatoes, garlic, cumin, and hot pepper sauce; set aside.

2 Trim fat from chops. Sprinkle both sides of chops with chili powder. In an extra-large skillet heat oil over medium-high heat. Add chops; cook 4 minutes or until browned, turning once. Remove chops, reserving drippings in skillet.

3 Add onions to reserved drippings; cook and stir over medium heat 3 minutes. Stir in corn mixture; top with chops. Bring to boiling; reduce heat. Simmer, covered, 10 to 12 minutes or until a thermometer registers 145°F.

4 Sprinkle chops with cilantro, if desired, and serve with hot cooked rice.

PER SERVING 396 **CAL**; 10 g **FAT** (2 g **SAT**); 107 mg **CHOL**; 369 mg **SODIUM**; 32 g **CARB**; 2 g **FIBER**; 42 g **PRO**

Crunchy Peanut Pork Lettuce Wraps

These low-carb pork and lettuce wraps work as an entrée for a light dinner or as an appetizer or first course—depending on how many of them you eat.

MAKES 4 servings **START TO FINISH** 25 minutes

Nonstick cooking spray
- 1   **teaspoon canola oil**
- 1   **clove garlic, minced**
- 1   **pound natural pork loin, trimmed of fat and cut into thin strips**
- ⅛   **teaspoon black pepper**
- 2   **tablespoons water**
- 2   **tablespoons peanut butter**
- 2   **tablespoons reduced-sodium soy sauce**
- ½   **tablespoon grated fresh ginger**
- 1   **teaspoon Asian chili sauce (sriracha sauce)**
- ½   **teaspoon apple cider vinegar**
- 1   **8-ounce can sliced water chestnuts, drained, rinsed, and chopped**
- ¼   **cup shredded carrot**
- ¼   **cup thinly sliced green onions**
- 3   **tablespoons roasted and salted peanuts, chopped**
- 12   **large butterhead (Boston or bibb) lettuce leaves**

1 Coat a large nonstick skillet with cooking spray, add oil and heat over medium-high heat.

2 Cook garlic in the hot oil 30 seconds. Add pork to the skillet and sprinkle with black pepper. Cook 5 minutes or until pork is no longer pink, turning once.

3 In a small bowl whisk together the water, peanut butter, soy sauce, ginger, chili sauce, and vinegar; pour over pork in hot skillet. Stir in water chestnuts, carrot, onions, and peanuts. Heat through.

4 Spoon about ¼ cup pork filling onto leaves. Top with green onions.

PER SERVING 274 **CAL**; 14 g **FAT** (3 g **SAT**); 63 mg **CHOL**; 391 mg **SODIUM**; 7 g **CARB**; 2 g **FIBER**; 30 g **PRO**

Southwestern Meat Loaf

For an extra-lean meat loaf, use ground turkey that is made only from breast meat. It may be a little drier than a blend of ground white and dark meat, but it will be lower in fat.

MAKES 8 servings **PREP** 30 minutes **COOL** 20 minutes **BAKE** 1 hour 45 minutes **STAND** 10 minutes

¼ **cup chopped onion**
1 **tablespoon vegetable oil**
½ **cup uncooked long grain rice**
4 **cloves garlic, minced**
1 **cup beef broth**
1 **15-ounce can black beans, rinsed and drained**
1½ **pounds ground turkey**
¾ **cup frozen or canned whole kernel corn, thawed or drained**
¾ **cup picante sauce**
½ **cup crushed tortilla chips or corn chips**
2 **teaspoons taco seasoning**
  Toppings, such as picante sauce, shredded Mexican four-cheese blend, sliced fresh jalapeño pepper, (tip, page 11), and/or snipped fresh cilantro (optional)
  Lime wedges (optional)

1 In a large saucepan cook onion in hot oil over medium heat 5 minutes or until tender, stirring occasionally. Stir in rice and garlic. Cook and stir 5 minutes or until rice is golden. Add broth. Bring to boiling; reduce heat. Simmer, covered, 10 to 15 minutes or until rice is tender. Stir in beans. Remove from heat; cool about 20 minutes.

2 Preheat oven to 350°F. In a large bowl combine ground turkey, corn, the ¾ cup picante sauce, crushed chips, and taco seasoning. Stir in rice mixture. Lightly pat mixture into a 9×5×3-inch loaf pan.

3 Bake 1¾ hours or until a thermometer registers 165°F. Let stand 10 minutes before serving. If desired, top with additional picante sauce, cheese, jalapeño pepper, and/or cilantro. If desired, serve with lime wedges.

PER SERVING 279 **CAL**; 10 g **FAT** (2 g **SAT**); 59 mg **CHOL**; 603 mg **SODIUM**; 28 g **CARB**; 3 g **FIBER**; 22 g **PRO**

Pork- and Corn-Stuffed Poblanos with Green Chile Cheese Sauce

Poblano peppers—the chiles used most often for chiles rellenos, the Mexican dish of cheese-stuffed, deep-fried peppers—can sometimes have a touch of heat but are usually quite mild.

MAKES 4 servings **PREP** 25 minutes **BROIL** 10 minutes **STAND** 20 minutes **BAKE** 20 minutes

4	large fresh poblano chile peppers (5 to 6 ounces each) (tip, page 11)
	Nonstick cooking spray
8	ounces extra-lean ground pork or uncooked ground turkey breast
½	cup chopped onion
½	cup no-salt-added canned black beans, rinsed and drained
½	cup no-salt-added canned whole kernel corn, rinsed and drained
½	cup salsa
1	teaspoon ground ancho chile pepper
½	teaspoon dried oregano, crushed
¼	teaspoon ground cumin
⅛	teaspoon ground cinnamon
1	4-ounce can diced green chile peppers, undrained
1	tablespoon butter
1	tablespoon all-purpose flour
½	cup fat-free milk
¼	cup shredded Monterey Jack cheese
	Paprika
	Fresh cilantro leaves (optional)

1 Preheat broiler. Keeping peppers whole, remove stems and seeds from poblano peppers. Place peppers on a foil-lined baking sheet. Broil 3 to 4 inches from heat 5 to 6 minutes or until peppers are charred. Turn peppers over; broil 5 to 6 minutes more or until charred. Bring foil up around peppers and fold edges together to enclose. Let stand 15 minutes or until cool enough to handle. Peel off and discard skins.

2 Meanwhile, coat a large nonstick skillet with cooking spray; heat skillet over medium heat. Add ground pork and onion; cook until meat is browned. Drain off any fat. Stir in black beans, corn, salsa, ground ancho pepper, oregano, cumin, and cinnamon. Cook 5 minutes or until heated through. Remove from heat; cover and keep warm.

3 Preheat oven to 375°F. Coat a 2-quart rectangular baking dish with cooking spray. Set aside. For sauce, place diced green chile peppers in a food processor; cover and process until smooth. In a small saucepan melt butter over medium heat. Stir in flour until smooth. Gradually stir in milk. Cook and stir until thickened and bubbly. Stir in pureed chiles and cheese. Cook and stir until cheese is melted and sauce is smooth.

4 To stuff poblano peppers, cut each pepper open from stem end to tip. Place each pepper, open side up, in prepared baking dish. Spoon about ⅔ cup meat filling along center of each pepper. Fold up sides, leaving some of the filling exposed. Pour sauce over stuffed peppers.

5 Bake, covered, 20 to 25 minutes or until heated through. Sprinkle generously with paprika. Let stand 5 minutes before serving. If desired, sprinkle with cilantro.

PER SERVING 272 **CAL**; 9 g **FAT** (4 g **SAT**); 48 mg **CHOL**; 401 mg **SODIUM**; 29 g **CARB**; 5 g **FIBER**; 22 g **PRO**

Eggplant, Fennel, and Sausage with Ziti

A small amount of Italian sausage flavors this dish while low-fat, low-calorie eggplant contributes a toothsome, meaty texture.

MAKES 6 servings **PREP** 30 minutes **SLOW COOK** 6 hours (low) or 3 hours (high) + 40 minutes (high) **STAND** 5 minutes

- 4 ounces bulk sweet Italian sausage
- 4 cups peeled and chopped eggplant
- 2 medium fennel bulbs, trimmed, cored, and thinly sliced
- 1 14.5-ounce can crushed fire-roasted tomatoes
- ½ cup water
- ¼ cup dry white wine
- 2 tablespoons tomato paste
- 2 cloves garlic, minced
- 1 teaspoon dried Italian seasoning, crushed
- 6 to 8 ounces dried cut ziti or penne pasta
- ½ cup snipped fresh basil
- 1 cup shredded part-skim mozzarella cheese (4 ounces)
  Snipped fresh basil

1 In a large skillet cook sausage over medium-high heat until browned. Drain off fat.

2 In a 5- to 6-quart slow cooker combine sausage, eggplant, fennel, tomatoes, the water, wine, tomato paste, garlic, and Italian seasoning. Cover and cook on low 6 to 7 hours or high 3 to 3½ hours.

3 If cooking on low, turn cooker to high. Stir in pasta and the ½ cup basil. Cover and cook 30 minutes. Stir then sprinkle with cheese. Cover and cook 10 minutes more. Let stand, uncovered, 5 to 10 minutes before serving. Sprinkle with additional basil.

PER SERVING 255 **CAL**; 5 g **FAT** (3 g **SAT**); 18 mg **CHOL**; 479 mg **SODIUM**; 38 g **CARB**; 6 g **FIBER**; 14 g **PRO**

Jerk Chicken and Pineapple Slaw

The cool, crisp, sweet slaw is a lovely contrast to the hot, pleasantly spicy grilled chicken.

MAKES 4 servings **START TO FINISH** 25 minutes

3	heads baby bok choy, trimmed and thinly sliced
2	cups shredded red cabbage
½	fresh pineapple, peeled, cored, and chopped
2	tablespoons cider vinegar
4	teaspoons packed brown sugar
2	teaspoons all-purpose flour
2	teaspoons Jamaican jerk seasoning
4	skinless, boneless chicken breast halves (1 to 1¼ pounds total)

1 For pineapple slaw, in an extra-large bowl combine bok choy, cabbage, and pineapple. In a small bowl stir together vinegar and 2 teaspoons of the brown sugar. Drizzle over slaw; toss to coat. Set aside.

2 In a resealable plastic bag combine the remaining 2 teaspoons brown sugar, the flour, and jerk seasoning. Add chicken to bag. Close bag; shake to coat.

3 Grill chicken on greased grill pan over medium heat 8 to 12 minutes or until no longer pink (165°F), turning once. Serve chicken with pineapple slaw.

PER SERVING 238 **CAL**; 7 g **FAT** (1 g **SAT**); 72 mg **CHOL**; 350 mg **SODIUM**; 19 g **CARB**; 3 g **FIBER**; 27 g **PRO**

Roasted Poblano Chicken Wild Rice

Boston-area fitness enthusiast Areli Biggers says she uses her trusted cast-iron skillet, "Lola" almost every day. "I love to create and cook new dishes," she says. Her winning recipe in the 2014 "Get Wild with Wild Rice" contest sponsored by the Minnesota Cultivated Wild Rice Council earned her $500. Areli is "passionate about peppers," she says. "Ancho, mirasol, pasilla, jalapeño, serrano, poblano, chipotles, and habanero peppers are all a very big part of my kitchen."

MAKES 4 servings   **PREP** 20 minutes   **COOK** 10 minutes

½   **cup chopped onion**

1   **teaspoon minced garlic**

2   **tablespoons butter with canola oil**

1   **9-ounce package frozen Green Giant Steamers Niblets Corn (without sauce), prepared according to package directions**

1   **cup chopped cooked Gold'n Plump Extra Tender Boneless Skinless Chicken Breast Fillets**

1   **cup cooked wild rice***

2   **large poblano peppers, roasted and chopped** (tip, page 11)**

½   **cup Sargento Artisan Blends Shredded Authentic Mexican cheese**

¼   **cup chicken broth**

2   **tablespoons sour cream**
    Salt and black pepper
    Snipped fresh parsley (optional)

1 In a large skillet cook onion and garlic in hot butter over medium heat 5 minutes or until tender.

2 Add corn, chicken, wild rice, poblano peppers, cheese, broth, and sour cream to skillet. Heat through. Season to taste with salt and pepper. If desired, top servings with snipped fresh parsley.

* Thoroughly rinse 1 cup uncooked wild rice. In a medium saucepan bring 3 cups water to a boil; add rice. Return to a boil; reduce heat and simmer, covered, 50 minutes or just until rice puffs open. Fluff with a fork and cook an additional 5 minutes. Drain excess liquid. Makes about 3 cups.

** To roast poblanos, preheat oven to 425°F. Quarter two fresh poblano chile peppers lengthwise; remove stems, seeds, and membranes. Place pepper pieces, cut sides down, on a foil-lined baking sheet. Bake 20 to 25 minutes or until peppers are charred and very tender. Bring foil up around peppers and fold edges together to enclose. Let stand about 15 minutes or until cool enough to handle. Use a sharp knife to loosen edges of skins; gently pull off and discard skin.

PER SERVING 309 **CAL**; 13 g **FAT** (6 g **SAT**); 48 mg **CHOL**; 422 mg **SODIUM**; 32 g **CARB**; 3 g **FIBER**; 17 g **PRO**

Asian Orange Chicken Thighs with Cauliflower Rice

Add extra color to this dish with one of the eye-catching cauliflower varieties that comes in beautiful—and completely natural—hues of purple, green, and orange.

MAKES 4 servings **PREP** 25 minutes **BAKE** 30 minutes **COOK** 18 minutes

Nonstick cooking spray

2	**tablespoons sesame oil (not toasted)**
4	**large bone-in chicken thighs (about 2¼ pounds total), skin removed**
1	**tablespoon reduced-sodium soy sauce**
1	**teaspoon finely shredded orange peel**
1	**tablespoon orange juice**
1	**tablespoon rice vinegar**
1	**tablespoon packed brown sugar**
¼	**teaspoon crushed red pepper**
1	**teaspoon cornstarch**
4	**cups coarsely chopped cauliflower florets**
½	**teaspoon kosher salt**
⅛	**teaspoon black pepper**

Snipped fresh cilantro (optional)

1 Preheat oven to 375°F. Coat a 2-quart square baking dish with nonstick cooking spray. In an extra-large nonstick skillet heat 1 tablespoon of the sesame oil over medium-high heat. Add chicken to hot oil; cook 10 minutes, turning to brown evenly. Transfer chicken to prepared dish, arranging in a single layer. Drain and discard drippings from skillet.

2 For sauce, in a small bowl whisk together soy sauce, orange peel and juice, vinegar, brown sugar, crushed red pepper, 2 tablespoons cold water, and cornstarch; add to skillet. Cook and stir until thickened and bubbly; pour sauce over chicken thighs in dish.

3 Bake, uncovered, 30 minutes or until chicken is done (175°F).

4 Meanwhile, place cauliflower in a large food processor. Cover and pulse several times until cauliflower is evenly chopped into rice-size pieces.

5 Wipe out skillet. Heat remaining 1 tablespoon oil in skillet over medium-high heat; add the cauliflower, salt, and pepper. Cook 8 to 10 minutes or until caramelized flecks appear throughout, stirring occasionally. Serve chicken thighs with cauliflower rice. If desired, sprinkle with cilantro and additional orange zest.

PER SERVING 285 **CAL**; 13 g **FAT** (3 g **SAT**); 145 mg **CHOL**; 526 mg **SODIUM**; 9 g **CARB**; 2 g **FIBER**; 32 g **PRO**

Garlic Cashew Chicken Casserole

This Chinese-inspired dish has all of the flavors of a stir-fry baked into a comforting—and healthful—casserole.

MAKES 6 servings **PREP** 35 minutes **BAKE** 24 minutes

	Nonstick cooking spray
1	cup reduced-sodium chicken broth
¼	cup hoisin sauce
2	tablespoons grated fresh ginger
4	teaspoons cornstarch
½	teaspoon crushed red pepper
⅛	teaspoon black pepper
1	pound skinless, boneless chicken breast halves, cut into 1-inch strips
2	cups sliced bok choy
2	medium onions, cut into thin wedges
1	cup sliced celery
1	cup sliced carrots
¾	cup chopped green sweet pepper
6	cloves garlic, minced
2	cups cooked brown rice
1	cup chow mein noodles, coarsely broken
½	cup cashews
1	or 2 green onions thinly sliced lengthwise

1 Preheat oven to 400°F. Lightly coat a 2-quart rectangular baking dish with cooking spray; set aside.

2 For sauce, in a medium bowl stir together broth, hoisin sauce, ginger, cornstarch, crushed red pepper, and black pepper; set aside.

3 Lightly coat an extra-large skillet with cooking spray; heat over medium-high heat. Add chicken; cook and stir until lightly browned. Remove from skillet. Add bok choy, onion wedges, celery, carrots, and sweet pepper to skillet. Cook 3 to 4 minutes or until vegetables begin to soften, stirring occasionally. Add garlic; cook and stir 30 seconds. Stir sauce; add to skillet. Cook 3 minutes or until sauce is thickened and bubbly. Stir in chicken and cooked rice. Transfer mixture to prepared baking dish.

4 Bake, covered, 20 minutes or until heated through. Top with chow mein noodles and cashews. Bake, uncovered, 4 to 5 minutes more or until noodles and cashews are golden. Sprinkle with green onions.

PER SERVING 340 **CAL**; 10 g **FAT** (2 g **SAT**); 49 mg **CHOL**; 480 mg **SODIUM**; 40 g **CARB**; 4 g **FIBER**; 23 g **PRO**

Roasted Salmon with Tomatoes and Corn

Serve this summery salmon dish with a crisp green salad and sourdough bread.

MAKES 4 servings **PREP** 25 minutes **ROAST** 15 minutes

Nonstick cooking spray

1	**1-pound fresh or frozen salmon fillet, skinned if desired**
½	**teaspoon salt**
½	**teaspoon black pepper**
2	**cups halved grape or cherry tomatoes**
2	**cups frozen or fresh whole kernel corn**
2	**teaspoons olive oil**
1	**teaspoon chili powder**
½	**teaspoon ground cumin**
½	**teaspoon finely shredded lime peel**
1	**tablespoon lime juice**
1	**teaspoon honey**
¼	**cup finely chopped red onion**
2	**tablespoons snipped fresh cilantro**
	Fresh cilantro leaves

1 Thaw salmon, if frozen. Rinse fish and pat dry with paper towels. Preheat oven to 400°F. Line a 15×10×1-inch baking pan with foil; coat foil with nonstick cooking spray. Place salmon in prepared pan. Sprinkle salmon with ¼ teaspoon each of the salt and pepper.

2 In a medium bowl combine tomatoes, corn, olive oil, chili powder, cumin, and remaining salt and pepper. Toss to coat. Spread tomato mixture around salmon in pan. Roast, uncovered, 15 to 18 minutes or until salmon flakes easily when tested with a fork.

3 Meanwhile, for the glaze, in a small bowl stir together lime peel, lime juice, and honey.

4 Using two large pancake turners, transfer salmon to a platter. Brush salmon with the glaze. Add onion and snipped cilantro to tomatoes in pan, stirring gently to combine. Top salmon with tomato mixture and cilantro leaves.

PER SERVING 285 **CAL**; 11 g **FAT** (2 g **SAT**); 62 mg **CHOL**; 360 mg **SODIUM**; 24 g **CARB**; 3 g **FIBER**; 26 g **PRO**

Baked Shrimp and Rice

This elegant-enough-for-company shrimp dish tastes deceptively indulgent. The rich and creamy texture comes from cream of shrimp soup and just a splash of half-and-half or light cream.

MAKES 6 servings **PREP** 30 minutes **BAKE** 30 minutes

- **12** ounces fresh or frozen, peeled and deveined cooked shrimp
- **2** tablespoons butter
- **½** cup chopped onion
- **¼** cup chopped green or red sweet pepper
- **2** cups cooked white rice
- **1** 10.75-ounce can condensed cream of shrimp or cream of celery soup
- **½** cup half-and-half or light cream
- **2** tablespoons dry sherry
- **1** teaspoon lemon juice
- **¼** teaspoon salt
- **⅛** teaspoon cayenne pepper
- **3** tablespoons sliced almonds, toasted (tip, page 8)
  Snipped fresh cilantro

1 Thaw shrimp, if frozen. Preheat oven to 350°F. In a large saucepan melt butter over medium heat. Add onion and sweet pepper; cook until tender, stirring occasionally. Remove from heat.

2 Stir shrimp, cooked rice, soup, half-and-half, sherry, lemon juice, salt, and cayenne pepper into vegetables. Transfer to a 2-quart square baking dish.

3 Bake, uncovered, 30 minutes or until heated through. Sprinkle with almonds and cilantro.

PER SERVING 290 **CAL**; 13 g **FAT** (5 g **SAT**); 141 mg **CHOL**; 624 mg **SODIUM**; 23 g **CARB**; 1 g **FIBER**; 19 g **PRO**

Greek Tuna Casserole

Artichoke hearts, feta cheese, oregano, and ripe olives lend great Mediterranean flavor to this quick-to-fix casserole featuring healthful canned tuna.

MAKES 6 servings **PREP** 20 minutes **ROAST** 15 minutes **BAKE** 40 minutes

Nonstick cooking spray
- ⅓ **cup dried whole wheat orzo pasta**
- 1 **medium eggplant, ends trimmed, cut into 1-inch-thick slices**
- 1 **large red sweet pepper, stemmed, quartered, and seeded**
- 2 **tablespoons olive oil**
- 1½ **teaspoons finely shredded lemon peel**
- 2 **tablespoons lemon juice**
- 1 **clove garlic, minced**
- 4 **tablespoons snipped fresh oregano**
- ½ **teaspoon salt**
- ¼ **teaspoon black pepper**
- ½ **cup panko bread crumbs**
- 3 **5-ounce cans very-low-sodium tuna (water pack), undrained, large pieces broken up**
- 1 **9-ounce package frozen artichoke hearts, thawed and quartered if needed**
- ½ **cup ripe olives, halved**
- ¼ **cup crumbled feta cheese**
Lemon wedges (optional)

1 Preheat oven to 425°F. Coat a 1½-quart gratin dish with cooking spray; set aside. Cook pasta according to package directions. Drain and set aside.

2 Line a 15×10×1-inch baking pan with foil. Lightly coat both sides of each eggplant slice with cooking spray. Place coated eggplant slices in prepared baking pan. Add sweet pepper quarters to pan with eggplant. Roast, uncovered, 15 to 20 minutes or just until eggplant begins to brown and peppers are tender. Remove from oven; let cool. Cut eggplant and pepper pieces into ¾-inch cubes. Reduce oven temperature to 350°F.

3 For lemon dressing, in a small bowl whisk together olive oil, 1 teaspoon of the lemon peel, the lemon juice, and garlic. Whisk in 3 tablespoons of the oregano, the salt, and black pepper; set aside. In another small bowl stir together panko, remaining oregano, and remaining lemon peel; set aside.

4 In a large bowl combine cooked orzo, eggplant, sweet pepper, tuna, artichoke hearts, olives, and feta cheese. Stir in the lemon dressing. Spoon into the prepared baking dish. Cover with foil. Bake 35 to 40 minutes or until heated through. Sprinkle seasoned panko over top. Bake, uncovered, 5 to 8 minutes more or until panko is golden brown. If desired, serve with lemon wedges.

PER SERVING 239 **CAL**; 8 g **FAT** (2 g **SAT**); 37 mg **CHOL**; 436 mg **SODIUM**; 24 g **CARB**; 9 g **FIBER**; 20 g **PRO**

Pinto Bean Burgers

Crushed baked tortilla chips give each bite of these crusty-on-the-outside, creamy-on-the-inside bean burgers a pleasant crunch.

MAKES 6 servings **PREP** 25 minutes **GRILL** 8 minutes

- **2**   **15- to 16-ounce cans pinto beans or no-salt-added pinto beans, rinsed and drained**
- **1**   **egg, lightly beaten**
- **½**   **cup fine dry bread crumbs**
- **½**   **cup salsa**
- **1**   **teaspoon chili powder**
- **½**   **teaspoon ground cumin**
- **¼**   **teaspoon salt**
- **½**   **cup coarsely crushed baked tortilla chips**
     Nonstick cooking spray
- **3**   **8-inch pita bread rounds, halved crosswise**
     Shredded lettuce
- **12**   **slices tomato**
     Salsa (optional)
     Sliced fresh jalapeños (tip, page 11) (optional)

1 Reserve 1 cup of the pinto beans; set aside. Place remaining beans in a food processor. Cover and process until smooth. (Or place remaining beans in a large bowl and mash with a potato masher or fork.)

2 In a large bowl combine egg, bread crumbs, the ½ cup salsa, chili powder, cumin, and salt. Add the reserved beans and pureed beans; mix well. Stir in crushed chips. Shape mixture into twelve ½-inch-thick patties. Coat both sides of patties with cooking spray.

3 Grill patties, covered, on a greased grill rack or grill pan over medium-high heat 8 minutes or until heated through (160°F), turning once.

4 Top pita halves with lettuce, tomato, 2 patties, and, if desired, additional salsa and chile peppers.

PER SERVING 283 **CAL**; 5 g **FAT** (1 g **SAT**); 31 mg **CHOL**; 710 mg **SODIUM**; 49 g **CARB**; 3 g **FIBER**; 12 g **PRO**

Greek Spinach-Pasta Salad with Feta and Beans

Baby spinach is perfect for using in salads because it doesn't require stemming. Here, the warm pasta and a little bit of the cooking water wilts the spinach just slightly.

MAKES 6 servings   **PREP** 25 minutes

1	5- to 6-ounce package fresh baby spinach
1	15-ounce can great Northern beans, rinsed and drained
1	cup crumbled feta cheese (4 ounces)
¼	cup dried tomatoes (not oil-packed), snipped
¼	cup chopped green onions
2	cloves garlic, minced
1	teaspoon finely shredded lemon peel
2	tablespoons lemon juice
2	tablespoons extra virgin olive oil
1	tablespoon snipped fresh oregano
1	tablespoon snipped fresh lemon thyme or thyme
½	teaspoon kosher salt or sea salt
½	teaspoon freshly ground black pepper
12	ounces dried cavatappi or farfalle pasta
	Shaved Parmesan or Pecorino Romano cheese

1 In a large serving bowl combine spinach, beans, feta cheese, tomatoes, green onions, garlic, lemon peel, lemon juice, oil, oregano, thyme, salt, and pepper. Cover; let stand at room temperature while preparing pasta.

2 Cook pasta according to package directions. Drain, reserving ¼ cup of the cooking water. Toss cooked pasta and pasta water with spinach salad. Serve warm or at room temperature. Top with shaved Parmesan cheese.

PER SERVING 408 **CAL**; 10 g **FAT** (4 g **SAT**); 19 mg **CHOL**; 487 mg **SODIUM**; 62 g **CARB**; 6 g **FIBER**; 17 g **PRO**

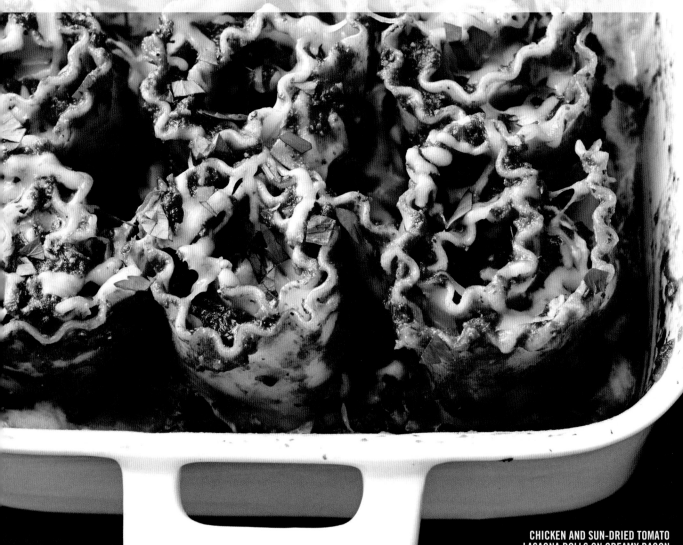

potluck pleasers

Any one of these dishes will be the most popular at the party.

CHICKEN AND SUN-DRIED TOMATO
LASAGNA ROLLS ON CREAMY BACON
PESTO BÉCHAMEL

APPETIZERS, BREADS, AND BEVERAGES

MAIN DISHES

SIDE DISHES

Hamburger Steak Sliders

Set out the spreads and toppings and let guests build a baby-size burger that suits their tastes perfectly.

MAKES 12 servings **PREP** 25 minutes **GRILL** 8 minutes

½	**cup very finely chopped red onion**
¼	**cup beef broth or water**
2	**tablespoons snipped fresh parsley (optional)**
2	**tablespoons steak sauce or barbecue sauce or 1 tablespoon Worcestershire sauce**
1	**tablespoon Dijon or coarse-grain mustard**
½	**teaspoon freshly ground black pepper**
12	**ounces ground beef sirloin (90% lean)**
12	**ounces ground beef chuck (85% lean)**
12	**whole grain cocktail-size hamburger buns or small round dinner rolls, split**
	Assorted spreads, such as barbecue sauce, steak sauce, ketchup, mustard, and/or mayonnaise
	Assorted toppings, such as cheese slices, tomato slices, torn lettuce, fresh basil leaves, cooked bacon, sliced red onion, and/or pickle relish (optional)

1 In a large bowl combine onion, broth, parsley (if desired), steak sauce, mustard, and pepper. Add ground sirloin and chuck; lightly mix together just until combined (do not overmix). Divide meat mixture into 12 portions and shape into ½-inch-thick patties.

2 Grill patties, covered, on a greased rack directly over medium heat 8 to 10 minutes or until done (160°F), turning once. Wrap buns in heavy foil and add to grill the last 5 minutes of grilling, turning once. Serve sliders with assorted spreads and toppings.

PER SERVING 193 **CAL**; 8 g **FAT** (3 g **SAT**); 38 mg **CHOL**; 269 mg **SODIUM**; 16 g **CARB**; 2 g **FIBER**; 14 g **PRO**

Pizza Pasta Skillet Casserole

Two favorite foods come together in one cheesy, savory, and saucy dish that will quickly become a family favorite.

MAKES 8 servings **PREP** 35 minutes **BAKE** 35 minutes

2	cups dried cavatappi (cellentani) pasta
1	3½-ounce package thinly sliced pepperoni
1	pound lean ground beef or sweet or hot Italian sausage
⅓	cup finely chopped onion
1	8-ounce package mushrooms, sliced
1	15-ounce can pizza sauce
1	8-ounce can tomato sauce
1	6-ounce can tomato paste
½	teaspoon sugar
⅛	teaspoon black pepper
⅛	teaspoon garlic salt
⅛	teaspoon onion salt
2	cups shredded mozzarella cheese
1	tablespoon grated Parmesan cheese

1 Preheat oven to 350°F. Cook pasta according to package directions, except omit the salt; drain. Return drained pasta to pot.

2 Meanwhile, cut three-fourths of the pepperoni slices in quarters; set aside.

3 In a large oven-going skillet cook ground beef, onion, and mushrooms until meat is browned and onion is tender; drain off fat.

4 Stir in the quartered pepperoni slices, the pizza sauce, tomato sauce, tomato paste, sugar, pepper, garlic salt, and onion salt. Add beef mixture to the cooked, drained pasta in the pot. (Do not rinse skillet.) Stir to combine.

5 Return half the pasta-beef mixture to the skillet. Sprinkle with half the mozzarella cheese. Repeat layers. Top with the whole pepperoni slices and sprinkle with the Parmesan cheese.

6 Bake 35 minutes or until casserole is heated through and cheese and pepperoni are lightly browned.

PER SERVING 387 **CAL**; 19 g **FAT** (8 g **SAT**); 67 mg **CHOL**; 916 mg **SODIUM**; 29 g **CARB**; 3 g **FIBER**; 28 g **PRO**

Chicken and Sun-Dried Tomato Lasagna Rolls on Creamy Bacon Pesto Béchamel

Mary Shivers of Ada, Oklahoma, says her mother was the best cook she has ever known. "I owe my passion and love of cooking to her," Mary says. "Her kitchen was always open and she encouraged me to get in there, explore, and develop my culinary creativity!" That imagination helped win Mary the grand prize in the 2015 Bella Sun Luci recipe contest with these indulgent pasta rolls.

MAKES 12 servings **PREP** 45 minutes **BAKE** 35 minutes

Nonstick cooking spray
¼ cup Bella Sun Luci Sun-Dried Tomato Pesto with Whole Pine Nuts, drained
2 tablespoons unsalted butter
½ teaspoon minced garlic
2 tablespoons all-purpose flour
1½ cups whole milk
¼ cup heavy cream
6 slices hickory smoked bacon, crisp-cooked and crumbled
¼ teaspoon salt
2 tablespoons Bella Sun Luci Extra Virgin Olive Oil
12 ounces boneless skinless chicken breasts, cut into ½-inch pieces
1 3.5-ounce pouch Bella Sun Luci Julienne Cut Sun-Dried Tomatoes
1 cup semi-packed fresh baby spinach, julienned
1 teaspoon minced garlic
½ teaspoon salt
1 large egg, beaten
1 15-ounce container whole milk ricotta cheese
⅓ cup grated aged Parmigiano-Reggiano cheese
½ teaspoon freshly ground black pepper
12 lasagna noodles, cooked according to package directions and lightly drizzled with olive oil
1 8.5-ounce jar Bella Sun Luci Sun-Dried Tomato Halves in Extra Virgin Olive Oil with Italian Herbs
1 8-ounce can roasted garlic tomato sauce
¼ cup chicken broth
¼ cup finely chopped fresh Italian parsley
1 teaspoon sugar
½ teaspoon salt
¼ teaspoon dried oregano
¼ teaspoon black pepper
1½ cups shredded mozzarella cheese
2 tablespoons snipped Italian parsley

1 Heat oven to 375°F. Lightly coat a 13×9×2-inch baking dish or lasagna pan with nonstick cooking spray. Set aside.

2 For the Béchamel, place pesto in a food processor; pulse until very finely chopped. In a medium saucepan combine butter and garlic over medium heat. Once butter is melted, stir in flour until smooth. Cook 2 minutes, stirring often. Slowly stir in milk. Cook until mixture begins to thicken. Whisk in cream. Remove from heat and stir in bacon, pesto, and salt. Spread evenly in prepared dish. Set aside.

3 For the lasagna rolls, heat the olive oil in a medium skillet over medium-high heat. Add chicken and cook 5 minutes or until no longer pink in the center (165°F), stirring occasionally. Stir in sun-dried tomatoes, spinach, garlic, and salt. Cook 1 minute, stirring often. Remove from heat and drain, if necessary.

4 In a medium bowl stir together egg, ricotta cheese, Parmigiano-Reggiano cheese, and pepper. Stir in chicken mixture.

5 Lay lasagna noodles on a work surface. Spread some of the chicken mixture on each noodle. Roll up, jelly-roll style, beginning at the narrow end. Arrange rolls, spiral sides up, on Béchamel.

6 For the sauce, in a food processor combine sun-dried tomato halves, tomato sauce, broth, parsley, sugar, salt, oregano, and pepper. Cover and process until sun-dried tomatoes are finely chopped. Spoon over lasagna rolls. Sprinkle with mozzarella cheese.

7 Coat one side of a sheet of foil with nonstick cooking spray then cover baking dish with foil, coated side down. Bake 30 to 35 minutes. Remove foil; bake 5 minutes more until cheese is melted and lasagna is heated through. Remove from oven and sprinkle with parsley.

PER SERVING 415 **CAL**; 21 g **FAT** (9 g **SAT**); 84 mg **CHOL**; 755 mg **SODIUM**; 34 g **CARB**; 4 g **FIBER**; 23 g **PRO**

Chicken Enchilada Pasta

Jumbo pasta shells are stuffed with a savory filling of chicken, enchilada sauce, refried beans, and taco seasoning in this recipe that combines Mexican flavors with Italian inspiration.

MAKES 8 servings **PREP** 40 minutes **BAKE** 35 minutes

1	12-ounce package dried jumbo shell macaroni
3¾	cups chopped green and/or red sweet peppers
1½	cups chopped red onions
1	fresh jalapeño, seeded and chopped (tip, page 11)
2	tablespoons vegetable oil
2	cups chopped cooked chicken (about 10 ounces)
2	10-ounce cans enchilada sauce
1	16-ounce can refried beans
½	1.25-ounce envelope taco seasoning mix (3 tablespoons)
¼	teaspoon salt
2	cups shredded Mexican four-cheese blend (8 ounces)
1	cup sliced green onions
2	cups nacho-flavor tortilla chips, crushed
	Sour cream and/or refrigerated guacamole

1 Preheat oven to 350°F. Cook jumbo shells according to package directions; drain. Rinse with cold water; drain again.

2 Meanwhile, in a large skillet cook sweet peppers, red onions, and jalapeño in hot oil over medium heat 5 minutes or until tender, stirring occasionally. Stir in chicken, ½ cup of the enchilada sauce, the refried beans, taco seasoning mix, and salt. Cook 5 minutes; stir in ½ cup of the cheese and ½ cup of the green onions.

3 Spread 1 cup of the remaining enchilada sauce in a 3-quart rectangular baking dish. Spoon chicken filling into cooked shells. Arrange filled shells in the baking dish. Drizzle with the remaining enchilada sauce.

4 Bake, covered, 30 minutes. Sprinkle with the remaining cheese. Bake, uncovered, 5 minutes or until cheese is melted. Sprinkle with tortilla chips and remaining green onions. Serve with sour cream and/or guacamole.

PER SERVING 520 **CAL**; 20 g **FAT** (8 g **SAT**); 56 mg **CHOL**; 1,338 mg **SODIUM**; 60 g **CARB**; 6 g **FIBER**; 27 g **PRO**

Tex-Mex Mac and Cheese

For a quick pico de gallo, combine 2 finely chopped medium tomatoes, 2 tablespoons finely chopped red onion, 2 tablespoons fresh snipped cilantro, and 1 seeded and finely chopped jalapeño.

MAKES 20 servings **PREP** 20 minutes **SLOW COOK** 5½ hours (low)

2	**pounds lean ground beef**
1	**cup chopped onion**
3	**cups shredded Mexican cheese blend (12 ounces)**
1	**16-ounce jar salsa**
1	**15-ounce jar process cheese dip**
1	**4-ounce can diced green chile peppers, undrained**
1	**2.25-ounce can sliced pitted black olives, drained**
12	**ounces dried elbow macaroni**
	Pico de gallo (optional)

1 In a large skillet cook ground beef and onion over medium-high heat until meat is browned. Drain off fat.

2 Transfer meat mixture to a 4½- to 6-quart slow cooker. Stir in Mexican cheese, salsa, cheese dip, undrained chile peppers, and drained olives.

3 Cover and cook on low 5½ to 6 hours.

4 Before serving, cook macaroni according to package directions; drain. Stir cooked macaroni into meat in cooker. If desired, top servings with pico de gallo.

PER SERVING 289 **CAL**; 16 g **FAT** (9 g **SAT**); 57 mg **CHOL**; 667 mg **SODIUM**; 18 g **CARB**; 1 g **FIBER**; 18 g **PRO**

Cheesy Brat Stew

This stir-and-bake casserole is perfect for busy nights when you need to bring a dish but have very little time to cook.

MAKES 8 servings   **PREP** 20 minutes   **BAKE** 45 minutes

6	fully cooked Polish sausage or bratwurst, cut into ½-inch pieces
4	medium potatoes, cooked, peeled, and cubed (1¼ pounds)
1	16-ounce package frozen cut green beans, thawed and drained
1	10¾-ounce can cream of mushroom soup
1	cup shredded cheddar cheese
⅓	cup chopped onion

1 Preheat oven to 350°F. In a 3-quart casserole dish stir together the sausage, potatoes, green beans, soup, cheddar cheese, and onion.

2 Bake, covered, 45 minutes or until heated through.

PER SERVING 732 **CAL**; 56 g **FAT** (21 g **SAT**); 134 mg **CHOL**; 1,987 mg **SODIUM**; 26 g **CARB**; 3 g **FIBER**; 30 g **PRO**

Southwest Corn Pudding

This homey side dish made with fresh or frozen corn, cream-style corn, green chiles, and sharp cheddar is a potluck staple that works for any type of gathering.

MAKES 10 servings **PREP** 25 minutes **BAKE** 30 minutes

1	tablespoon olive oil
1	tablespoon butter
1	medium onion, halved and thinly sliced
1½	cups fresh corn kernels (3 ears), or thawed frozen whole kernel corn
½	cup chopped red sweet pepper
½	teaspoon ground cumin
¼	cup cornmeal
2	tablespoons all-purpose flour
½	teaspoon salt
1	14.5-ounce can cream-style corn
4	eggs, lightly beaten
1	4-ounce can diced green chiles, undrained
1	cup shredded sharp cheddar cheese (4 ounces)
1	tablespoon butter

1 Preheat oven to 350°F. Heat oil and 1 tablespoon butter in a 9- or 10-inch cast-iron or other heavy oven-going skillet over medium-high heat. When butter is melted and begins to bubble, add onion. Cook 5 minutes or until onion is soft and beginning to brown, stirring occasionally. Add corn kernels, sweet pepper, and cumin. Cook and stir 3 minutes more. Remove skillet from heat to cool slightly.

2 Meanwhile, in a medium bowl combine cornmeal, flour, and salt. Add cream-style corn, eggs, chiles, and cheese; stir just until combined. Fold in onion mixture.

3 Return skillet to medium heat and add 1 tablespoon butter. When butter is melted, tilt skillet to coat bottom with butter. Pour batter into skillet; transfer to oven. Bake 30 to 35 minutes or until a knife inserted near center comes out clean. Serve warm.

PER SERVING 183 **CAL**; 10 g **FAT** (5 g **SAT**); 92 mg **CHOL**; 389 mg **SODIUM**; 18 g **CARB**; 1 g **FIBER**; 8 g **PRO**

Creamy Grits with Roasted Poblanos

Keep these creamy grits warm on low in the slow cooker for the duration of the party.

MAKES 8 servings **PREP** 25 minutes **ROAST** 20 minutes **STAND** 15 minutes **SLOW COOK** 3 hour (low) or 1½ hours (high)

3   **fresh poblano peppers (tip, page 11)**
2   **14.5-ounce cans reduced-sodium chicken broth**
2½   **cups water**
1½   **cups regular hominy grits**
¼   **teaspoon salt**
⅛   **teaspoon black pepper**
2   **cups shredded aged cheddar cheese (8 ounces)**
     Milk

1 Preheat oven to 425°F. Line a baking sheet with foil; set aside. Halve peppers lengthwise; remove stems, seeds, and membranes. Place peppers, cut sides down, on prepared baking sheet. Roast 20 to 25 minutes or until charred. Bring foil up around peppers to enclose. Let stand 15 minutes or until cool. Use a sharp knife to loosen edges of skins; gently pull off and discard skins. Cut peppers into 2-inch long, ¼-inch-wide strips.

2 In a 3½- or 4-quart slow cooker combine peppers, broth, the water, grits, salt, and pepper.

3 Cover and cook on low 3 to 3½ hours or on high 1½ to 1¾ hours or until a small amount of liquid is visible on top of grits.

4 Stir 1½ cups of the cheese into the cooked grits; stir until cheese is melted. If grits become too thick, thin with milk to desired consistency. Top each serving with some of the remaining cheese.

PER SERVING 254 **CAL**; 10 g **FAT** (6 g **SAT**); 31 mg **CHOL**; 497 mg **SODIUM**; 29 g **CARB**; 2 g **FIBER**; 12 g **PRO**

Ranch Beans with Peppered Bacon

If you are toting this dish to a potluck, bring the reserved bacon in a small container or resealable plastic bag and put it on top of the beans right before serving to keep it crispy and delicious.

MAKES 18 servings **PREP** 25 minutes **SLOW COOK** 6 hours (low) or 3 hours (high)

8	slices peppered bacon or regular bacon, cut in half crosswise
1	cup chopped onion
¾	cup chopped green sweet pepper
1	to 2 fresh jalapeños, seeded and finely chopped (tip, page 11)
3	cloves garlic, minced
1	cup stout beer
2	15-ounce cans white beans or navy beans, drained and rinsed
2	15-ounce cans pinto beans, drained and rinsed
1	cup barbecue sauce
½	cup packed brown sugar
½	cup cider vinegar
3	tablespoons Worcestershire sauce
3	tablespoons Dijon mustard

1 In a large skillet cook bacon over medium-low heat to remove some of the fat. (Do not cook until crisp.) Remove bacon and drain on paper towels; reserve 1 teaspoon drippings in skillet. Finely chop six of the bacon slices; reserve remaining bacon slices.

2 Add chopped bacon, onion, sweet pepper, jalapeño, and garlic to the reserved drippings. Cook and stir over medium-high heat 3 minutes. Add beer, stirring to scrape up crusty brown bits; simmer 2 to 3 minutes. Transfer to a 6-quart slow cooker.

3 Stir in white beans, pinto beans, barbecue sauce, brown sugar, vinegar, Worcestershire sauce, and mustard. Place reserved bacon on beans.

4 Cover and cook on low 6 to 8 hours or on high 3 to 4 hours.

PER SERVING 167 **CAL**; 2 g **FAT** (1 g **SAT**); 4 mg **CHOL**; 469 mg **SODIUM**; 29 g **CARB**; 5 g **FIBER**; 7 g **PRO**

Bavarian-Style Potato Salad

Serve this sweet-and-sour German-style potato salad chilled or at room temperature.

MAKES 6 servings **PREP** 20 minutes **COOK** 20 minutes

1½	**pounds Yukon Gold potatoes, well scrubbed**
¼	**cup white wine vinegar**
¾	**teaspoon kosher salt**
½	**teaspoon black pepper**
4	**slices bacon, cut into ¼-inch pieces**
½	**cup chopped red onion**
¼	**cup chicken broth**
2	**tablespoons vegetable oil**
1	**teaspoon sugar**
¾	**teaspoon dried dill**
½	**teaspoon celery seeds**
2	**tablespoons snipped fresh dill or fresh Italian parsley**

1 In a large saucepan cover potatoes in lightly salted water. Bring to boil. Reduce heat and simmer, covered, 20 to 25 minutes or just until tender; drain well. Rinse with cold water; cool slightly. Halve and cut potatoes into ¼-inch-thick slices; place in a large bowl. Drizzle warm potatoes with vinegar and season with the salt and pepper.

2 For dressing, in a large skillet cook bacon over medium heat until crisp. Remove skillet from heat. Add onion, broth, oil, sugar, dill, and celery seeds to bacon and drippings; stir well to combine. Pour dressing over potatoes; gently toss to coat. Sprinkle with fresh dill. Serve at room temperature or chilled.

PER SERVING 248 **CAL**; 16 g **FAT** (4 g **SAT**); 17 mg **CHOL**; 513 mg **SODIUM**; 20 g **CARB**; 3 g **FIBER**; 5 g **PRO**

Tomato Galette

Make this elegantly rustic tomato and cheese tart in mid- to late summer, at the height of tomato season.

MAKES 8 servings **PREP** 35 minutes **CHILL** 30 minutes **BAKE** 30 minutes **COOL** 10 minutes

½   **cup cold unsalted butter, cubed**
1½ **cups all-purpose flour**
⅓   **cup shredded Parmesan cheese**
1   **teaspoon cracked black pepper**
4   **to 6 tablespoons cold water**
4   **large heirloom tomatoes, cored (about 2 pounds)**
1   **teaspoon kosher salt**
3   **tablespoons fine dry bread crumbs**
½   **cup thinly sliced shallot**
2   **teaspoons fresh thyme leaves**
4   **to 6 ounces semisoft goat cheese (chèvre) or feta cheese, crumbled**
1   **egg, lightly beaten**
1   **tablespoon water**
     Fresh basil leaves (snip large leaves)

1 In a large bowl cut butter into flour with a pastry blender until pieces are pea size*. Stir in Parmesan and cracked pepper. Sprinkle 1 tablespoon cold water over part of mixture; toss with a fork. Push moistened dough to the side of bowl. Repeat, using 1 tablespoon of the water at a time, until all the dough is moistened. Form dough into a disk, wrap with plastic wrap and chill at least 30 minutes or until easy to handle (up to 24 hours).

2 Meanwhile, slice the tomatoes about ¼ inch thick and arrange on a wire rack over a baking pan, sink, or paper towels. Sprinkle with salt and let drain 30 minutes.

3 Preheat oven to 375°. On a lightly floured surface roll dough to a 13-inch circle. Fold in half to transfer to a large baking sheet lined with parchment paper; unfold.

4 Evenly spread bread crumbs on pastry, leaving a 2-inch border. Layer tomatoes, shallot, thyme, and goat cheese on bread crumbs. Fold crust over filling, pleating as necessary exposing some filling in center. Combine egg and 1 tablespoon water; brush on edges of pastry.

5 Bake 30 to 40 minutes or until crust is browned and crisp. Cool at least 10 minutes. Serve warm or at room temperature; sprinkle with fresh basil and cut into wedges.

*Food Processor Method: The first step can be done in the food processor. Place steel blade in food processor bowl; add flour and butter. Cover and pulse until pieces are pea size. Add Parmesan and pepper; pulse just until combined. Transfer to bowl and proceed as directed.

PER SERVING 300 **CAL**; 18 g **FAT** (11 g **SAT**); 67 mg **CHOL**; 414 mg **SODIUM**; 26 g **CARB**; 3 g **FIBER**; 9 g **PRO**

Smokehouse Cranberry Cheese Bread

Memories of visits to her in-laws in Vermont inspired this rich, brioche-like bread that earned Lisa Keys first place in the 2015 National Festival of Breads competition sponsored by the Kansas Wheat Commission. "My mother-in-law always had smoked cheeses from local farmers and fresh maple syrup tapped from trees in town," says the Pennsylvania baker. "She also introduced me to tofu in delicious breakfast smoothies. This honors all of her goodness."

MAKES 32 servings   **PREP** 45 minutes   **RISE** 1 hour 40 minutes   **BAKE** 35 minutes   **COOL** 2 minutes

---

2	packages Red Star Quick-Rise yeast
3	tablespoons warm water (110°F to 115°F)
2	tablespoons pure maple syrup
1	cup unsalted butter, softened (8 ounces)
½	cup firm silken-style tofu (fresh bean curd) (4 ounces) at room temperature
4	eggs at room temperature
2	cups shredded smoked Gouda or smoked cheddar cheese (8 ounces) at room temperature
1	teaspoon salt
½	teaspoon black pepper
4½ to 5	cups King Arthur unbleached bread flour
1	cup sweetened dried cranberries (5 ounces)

1 In a small bowl dissolve yeast in the water and maple syrup. Let stand 10 minutes or until foamy.

2 In the bowl of a stand mixer fitted with a paddle beat butter and tofu until light and fluffy, scraping sides of bowl as needed. Beat in eggs, one at a time. Stir in cheese, salt, pepper, yeast mixture, and 4 cups of the flour; blend well. Exchange paddle for dough hook.

3 Add cranberries to dough. Gradually add enough remaining flour until a soft dough forms. Knead dough on low to medium until smooth and elastic, (about 8 minutes).* Place dough in a lightly greased bowl, turning once to grease surface of dough. Cover; let rise in a warm place until double in size (about 1 hour).

4 Punch dough down. Turn out onto a lightly floured surface. Divide dough in half. Shape into two 6- to 7-inch round loaves. Place loaves in two buttered 9-inch round cake pans. Cover and let rise until doubled (40 to 45 minutes).

5 Meanwhile, preheat oven to 375°F. Uncover dough. Using a sharp knife, make a ¼-inch deep "X" across loaf.

6 Bake 35 minutes or until golden brown and an instant read thermometer registers 200°F. (If necessary, cover loosely with foil the last 15 minutes to prevent overbrowning). Cool in pans on wire racks 2 minutes. Remove bread from pans. Cool on wire racks.

* Hand-Mixer option As an alternative to a stand mixer with a paddle and dough hook, in a large bowl combine butter and tofu. Beat with a hand mixer on medium until light and fluffy. Beat in eggs, one at time. Stir in cheese, salt, pepper, yeast mixture, and as much of 4 cups of the flour as you can with the mixer. Stir in any of the remaining 4 cups flour and the cranberries. Turn dough out onto a lightly floured surface. Knead in enough of the remaining flour to make a moderately stiff dough that is smooth and elastic (6 to 8 minutes). Shape dough into a ball. Place in a lightly greased bowl, turning to grease surface of dough. Cover; let rise in warm place until double in size (about 1 hour). Continue with Step 4.

PER SERVING 173 **CAL**; 9 g **FAT** (5 g **SAT**); 47 mg **CHOL**; 143 mg **SODIUM**; 18 g **CARB**; 1 g **FIBER**; 5 g **PRO**

Loco Cocoa

The "loco" or "crazy" in this cocoa is how deliciously rich it is—and how easy it is to prepare in the slow cooker. Try one of the variations, including a minty version for the holidays, a spiced Mexican-style cocoa, and a kid-friendly peanut butter-flavor variation with a fun "paint splatter" of hot fudge ice cream topping.

MAKES 12 servings **PREP** 10 minutes **SLOW COOK** 5 hours (low) or 2½ hours (high)

1	**cup premium unsweetened cocoa powder**
¼	**to ⅓ cup sugar**
¼	**teaspoon salt**
½	**cup hot water**
4	**cups half-and-half or light cream**
4	**cups whole milk**
⅓	**cup bittersweet chocolate pieces or 2 ounces bittersweet chocolate, chopped**
2	**teaspoons vanilla**

1 In a 3- or 4-quart slow cooker combine cocoa, sugar, and salt. Stir in the hot water to form a paste. Whisk in half-and-half and milk.

2 Cover and cook on low 5 to 6 hours or on high 2½ to 3 hours. Do not let boil. Whisk in bittersweet chocolate until melted.

3 If necessary, skim "skin" from surface and discard. Stir in vanilla. Serve immediately or keep warm, covered, on warm or low up to 2 hours.

PER SERVING 211 **CAL**; 15 g **FAT** (9 g **SAT**); 38 mg **CHOL**; 115 mg **SODIUM**; 18 g **CARB**; 3 g **FIBER**; 7 g **PRO**

Insane Candy Cane Cocoa Prepare as directed, except omit vanilla. To serve, stir in 2 teaspoons peppermint extract. Ladle into mugs. Top each serving with sweetened whipped cream and a sprinkle of crushed peppermint candies. Serve with small candy canes.

Mexican Marshmallow Cocoa Prepare as directed, except add 8 inches of stick cinnamon; 1 vanilla bean, cut in half lengthwise; and ⅛ to ¼ teaspoon ground ancho chile pepper, chili powder, or cayenne pepper along with half-and-half and milk. To serve, omit vanilla and use a slotted spoon to remove vanilla bean and cinnamon sticks. Stir in ¼ teaspoon almond extract. In a small bowl combine 3 tablespoons unsweetened cocoa powder, 1 teaspoon powdered sugar, and ¼ teaspoon ground cinnamon. Roll 12 large marshmallows in cocoa powder mixture. Ladle hot cocoa into mugs; top each with a cocoa-coated marshmallow.

Splatter Paint Cocoa Prepare as directed, except stir ¼ cup creamy peanut butter into the cocoa before adding half-and-half and milk. About 30 minutes before serving, microwave ¼ to ½ cup hot fudge ice cream topping on high 30 seconds; stir. Use a spoon to splatter the warm topping around insides of glass mugs or thick-sided clear glasses; let topping set up. Carefully ladle hot cocoa into mugs or glasses.

CHAPTER 8

handheld favorites

Sandwiches, wraps, pizzas, and calzones tailor-made for casual eating.

ROASTED PEPPER-CHEESE MELTS

CALZONES, PIZZAS, AND FLATBREADS

SANDWICHES, TACOS, AND FISH AND CHIPS

The Sports Bar

Gourmet hot wings at the favorite sports bar of Stefanie and Chris Schaldenbrand of Santa Ana, California, inspired this champion sandwich at the 2015 Grilled Cheese Academy Recipe Showdown sponsored by the Wisconsin Milk Marketing Board. It features shredded chicken smothered in zesty BBQ sauce, creamy gorgonzola fondue with gooey mozzarella, and a crunchy carrot-celery slaw on crisp-grilled mustard-coated bread. Share one with a friend.

MAKES 4 servings **START TO FINISH** 45 minutes

¼ **cup mayonnaise**
1 **tablespoon spicy mustard**
2 **medium carrots, shredded**
2 **stalks celery, finely chopped**
1 **tablespoon fresh lemon juice**
¾ **cup ketchup**
¼ **cup packed brown sugar**
¼ **tablespoon sriracha sauce**
2 **tablespoons honey**
1 **tablespoon soy sauce**
1 **teaspoon garlic powder**
¾ **teaspoon salt**
½ **cup light beer**
1½ **pounds boneless, skinless chicken thighs**
2 **tablespoons extra virgin olive oil**
Salt and black pepper
4 **tablespoons butter**
1 **clove garlic, minced**
2 **tablespoons all-purpose flour**
2 **tablespoons dry vermouth**
¾ **cup half-and-half or light cream**
6 **ounces Wisconsin Gorgonzola cheese, rumbled (1 cup)**
4 **slices sourdough bread**
4 **ounces Wisconsin mozzarella cheese, shredded (1 cup)**

1 In a small bowl combine mayonnaise and mustard. In another bowl toss carrots and celery with lemon juice.

2 For the sriracha barbecue sauce, in a small saucepan combine ketchup, brown sugar, sriracha sauce, honey, soy sauce, garlic powder, and salt. Bring to a boil; stir in beer. Reduce heat and simmer, uncovered, 15 minutes or until sauce is slightly thickened.

3 For the chicken, preheat oven to 425°F. Brush chicken with 1 tablespoon of the oil and season with salt and pepper. In a 10-inch cast-iron skillet heat remaining 1 tablespoon oil. Add chicken and cook 5 minutes or until browned on both sides, turning once. Add sriracha barbecue sauce to skillet. Place skillet in the oven and bake 15 minutes or until a thermometer registers 160°F. Remove chicken from oven; transfer to a plate to cool slightly. Shred chicken with two forks; return shredded chicken to skillet and toss with sauce. Spread chicken in a single layer. Preheat broiler. Broil 4 to 5 inches from the heat 4 minutes or until caramelized and crusty.

4 For the Gorgonzola fondue, melt 3 tablespoons of the butter in a small saucepan over medium-low heat. Add garlic; cook 1 minute or until lightly browned (be careful not to burn garlic). Stir in flour; cook 1 minute. Stir in vermouth. Add half-and-half, continuing to stir until sauce begins to thicken. Bring sauce to boiling. Reduce heat; gradually add Gorgonzola, stirring until completely melted. Season to taste with salt and pepper.

5 Melt the remaining 1 tablespoon butter in a nonstick oven-going skillet over medium-low heat. Spread mayonnaise-mustard on one side of each slice of bread. Place two slices, mayonnaise sides up, in skillet. Cook over medium-high heat 2 to 3 minutes or until golden, turning once. Repeat with remaining bread slices. Place bread slices, mayonnaise sides up on baking sheet. Top with mozzarella cheese. Broil 4- to 5-inches from heat for 1 minute or until cheese is melted.

6 Divide the chicken between two slices. Generously drizzle with some of the Gorgonzola fondue. Add a heaping pile of carrot-celery. Top with bread slices, cheese sides down. Halve sandwiches for serving.

PER SERVING 1,137 **CAL**; 60 g **FAT** (26 g **SAT**); 263 mg **CHOL**; 2,969 mg **SODIUM**; 86 g **CARB**; 3 g **FIBER**; 61 g **PRO**

German Sausage Pretzel Sandwich

Use a little—or more—of the optional horseradish to give the creamy sauce for these hearty sandwiches head-clearing power. They're perfect with a cold beer on a fall football afternoon with friends.

MAKES 6 serving **START TO FINISH** 35 minutes

¼   **cup mayonnaise**
¼   **cup Dijon mustard**
¼   **cup whole grain mustard**
2   **tablespoons packed brown sugar**
2   **teaspoons cider vinegar**
2   **to 3 teaspoons prepared horseradish (optional)**
6   **uncooked bratwurst or other sausage links**
6   **pretzel hoagie rolls, split but not separated**
3   **tablespoons butter, melted**
6   **1-ounce slices Swiss cheese, halved diagonally**
½   **cup sauerkraut, rinsed and drained**
½   **cup dill pickle slices (optional)**

1 For the sauce, in a small bowl combine mayonnaise, Dijon mustard, whole grain mustard, brown sugar, vinegar, and, if desired, horseradish; set aside.

2 Cook bratwurst according to package directions (160°F); keep warm.

3 Brush cut sides of rolls with melted butter. Toast rolls, cut sides down, on a griddle or grill pan over medium heat until golden.

4 For each hoagie, place two half-slices of cheese on bottom of roll. Top with bratwurst, sauerkraut, and, if desired, pickles. Drizzle with 1 tablespoon of the sauce; replace tops of rolls. Pass remaining sauce.

PER SERVING 713 **CAL**; 44 g **FAT** (20 g **SAT**); 147 mg **CHOL**; 2,170 mg **SODIUM**; 49 g **CARB**; 2 g **FIBER**; 29 g **PRO**

New Orleans-Style Muffuletta

Some aficionados of the muffuletta say it's all about the olive relish. Let the relish marinate for at least 4 hours to blend the flavors. Muffulettas are perfect for parties because they can be made an hour or so ahead and can sit out on a serving platter for an hour or so as well.

MAKES 6 servings **PREP** 20 minutes **CHILL** 4 hours

½ cup coarsely chopped pitted ripe olives

½ cup chopped pimiento-stuffed green olives

1 tablespoon snipped fresh Italian parsley

2 teaspoons lemon juice

½ teaspoon dried oregano, crushed

1 tablespoon olive oil

1 clove garlic, minced

1 16-ounce ciabatta bread or French bread

6 lettuce leaves

3 ounces thinly sliced salami, pepperoni, or summer sausage

3 ounces thinly sliced cooked ham or turkey

6 ounces thinly sliced provolone, Swiss, or mozzarella cheese

1 to 2 medium tomatoes, thinly sliced

⅛ teaspoon coarse ground black pepper

1 For the olive relish, in a small bowl combine ripe olives, green olives, parsley, lemon juice, and oregano. Cover and chill at least 4 hours or up to 24 hours.

2 In a small bowl stir together oil and garlic; set aside. Cut bread in half horizontally. Using a spoon, hollow out the inside of the top half, leaving a ¾-inch shell.

3 Brush bottom half of bread with garlic oil. Layer with lettuce, meats, cheese, and tomatoes. Sprinkle tomatoes with pepper. Stir olive relish; mound on tomatoes. Replace top half of bread. Cut into six portions.

PER SERVING 435 **CAL**; 21 g **FAT** (8 g **SAT**); 41 mg **CHOL**; 1,512 mg **SODIUM**; 43 g **CARB**; 3 g **FIBER**; 20 g **PRO**

Chicken Caesar Egg Sandwich

The chicken for these tasty sandwiches can soak in the Caesar marinade and dressing for between 8 and 24 hours, making them a convenient option for a (mostly) make-ahead meal.

MAKES 4 servings **PREP** 25 minutes **MARINATE** 8 hours **COOK** 20 minutes

6	**cloves garlic, minced**
6	**anchovies, drained**
¼	**cup lemon juice**
½	**cup olive oil**
2	**tablespoons Dijon mustard**
2	**hard-cooked egg yolks**
1	**teaspoon sugar**
1	**teaspoon Worcestershire sauce**
⅛	**teaspoon black pepper**
2	**8- to 10-ounce skinless, boneless chicken breast halves**
	Nonstick cooking spray
4	**eggs**
4	**croissants, split**
8	**slices cooked bacon**
1	**cup shredded romaine lettuce**
	Shaved Parmesan cheese

1 For dressing, place garlic, anchovies, and lemon juice in a blender or food processor. Blend until nearly smooth, stopping to scrape down sides as needed. Add oil, mustard, cooked egg yolks, sugar, Worcestershire, and pepper. Blend until smooth. Reserve ¼ cup dressing; chill, covered, until needed. Set remaining dressing aside to be used as marinade.

2 Place each chicken breast half between two pieces of plastic wrap. Pound chicken lightly with the flat side of a meat mallet to about ½-inch thickness. Remove plastic wrap. Place chicken in a resealable plastic bag. Pour marinade over chicken; turn to coat. Marinate in refrigerator 8 hours or up to 24 hours, turning occasionally.

3 Drain chicken, discarding marinade. Coat a large nonstick skillet with cooking spray. Cook chicken over medium heat 4 to 6 minutes per side or until no longer pink (170°). Remove chicken; set aside. Wipe skillet clean.

4 Coat the skillet with cooking spray. Break eggs into skillet. Reduce heat to low; fry eggs 3 to 4 minutes or until whites are completely set and yolks begin to thicken. Turn eggs and cook 45 seconds to 1 minute more.

5 Slice chicken into bite-size strips and arrange on bottom half of each croissant. Layer eggs, bacon, lettuce, reserved dressing, and Parmesan cheese.

PER SERVING 564 **CAL**; 35 g **FAT** (10 g **SAT**); 339 mg **CHOL**; 1,040 mg **SODIUM**; 24 g **CARB**; 1 g **FIBER**; 37 g **PRO**

Korean Chicken Tacos

Bottled sweet and spicy Korean barbecue sauce is available at most large supermarkets (and big box stores that have food departments) as well as at Asian markets.

MAKES 4 servings **START TO FINISH** 25 minutes

3	tablespoons reduced-sodium soy sauce
1	tablespoon lime juice
2	teaspoons packed brown sugar
1½	teaspoons grated fresh ginger
2	cloves garlic, minced
1	teaspoon cornstarch
1	teaspoon Asian chili-garlic sauce
1	tablespoon vegetable oil
1½	pounds skinless, boneless chicken breast halves, cut into bite-size strips
1¼	cups kimchi
8	5- to 6-inch white corn tortillas, heated according to package directions
⅓	cup snipped fresh cilantro
	Korean barbecue sauce (optional)

1 For the sauce, in a small bowl combine soy sauce, lime juice, brown sugar, ginger, garlic, cornstarch, and chili-garlic sauce; set aside.

2 In a large skillet heat oil over medium heat. Add chicken; cook and stir 8 to 10 minutes or until no longer pink. Stir sauce; add to chicken. Cook and stir until thickened and bubbly.

3 Divide chicken and kimchi among warm tortillas. Top with cilantro and, if desired, serve with Korean barbecue sauce.

PER SERVING 354 **CAL**; 9 g **FAT** (1 g **SAT**); 109 mg **CHOL**; 790 mg **SODIUM**; 26 g **CARB**; 3 g **FIBER**; 39 g **PRO**

Niçoise Salad Sandwiches

This sandwich is inspired by salade niçoise—the south-of-France salad traditionally composed of tuna, slender French green beans, tomatoes, hard-cooked eggs, niçoise olives, and potatoes dressed in a lemony vinaigrette.

MAKES 4 servings **PREP** 20 minutes

12	**thin slices whole wheat bread, toasted**
4	**butterhead (Boston or bibb) lettuce leaves**
½	**cup very thin fresh green beans, trimmed**
2	**4.5-ounce pouches lemon-pepper marinated chunk light tuna***
1	**medium tomato, thinly sliced**
½	**medium red onion, thinly sliced**
2	**hard-cooked eggs, sliced (optional)**
¼	**cup Niçoise or kalamata olives, halved**
1	**recipe Fresh Parsley Gremolata Vinaigrette**

1 Layer four bread slices with lettuce, green beans, and tuna. Layer another four bread slices with tomato, red onion, egg slices (if desired), and olives. Drizzle the eight layered bread slices with Fresh Parsley Gremolata Vinaigrette.

2 Place tomato-layered slices on tuna-layered bread slices to make four stacks. Top stacks with the remaining four bread slices.

3 Cut each sandwich in half. Tightly wrap each sandwich in plastic wrap. If desired, chill up to 4 hours before serving.

Fresh Parsley Gremolata Vinaigrette In a screw-top jar combine ¼ cup vinegar, ¼ cup olive oil, 2 tablespoons snipped fresh Italian parsley, 2 cloves minced garlic, ½ teaspoon finely shredded lemon peel, ¼ teaspoon salt, and ¼ teaspoon cracked pepper. Cover and shake well.

*Tip If you can't find marinated tuna, squeeze a lemon wedge over drained regular tuna.

PER SERVING 367 CAL; 18 g FAT (3 g SAT); 28 mg CHOL; 652 mg SODIUM; 26 g CARB; 5 g FIBER; 25 g PRO

Roasted Pepper-Cheese Melts

This toasty vegetarian sandwich couldn't be quicker to make—and it features pantry staples such as roasted red peppers, pesto, bread, and cheese for a satisfying dinner on the fly.

MAKES 4 servings   **PREP** 20 minutes   **STAND** 15 minutes

- ¾ **cup bottled roasted red sweet pepper strips**
- 3 **tablespoons balsamic vinegar**
- 12 **ounces whole grain baguette-style French bread**
- ¼ **cup basil pesto**
- 6 **ounces thinly sliced provolone cheese or fresh mozzarella cheese**
  Nonstick cooking spray

1 In a small bowl combine roasted pepper strips and vinegar; toss gently to coat. Let stand 15 minutes; drain well.

2 Meanwhile, cut bread crosswise into four portions. Split each bread portion in half horizontally. Remove some soft bread from the inside of each half, leaving ½-inch shells.

3 Spread cut sides of bread with pesto. Place roasted pepper strips and cheese on bottoms of bread. Replace tops of bread, pesto sides down. Lightly coat outside of sandwiches with cooking spray.

4 Heat a nonstick grill pan over medium heat. Place sandwiches, half at a time if necessary, in pan. Weight with a heavy skillet and grill 2 minutes or until bread is toasted. Turn sandwiches, weight down again, and grill 1 to 2 minutes or until bread is toasted and filling is heated through.

PER SERVING 457 **CAL**; 23 g **FAT** (9 g **SAT**); 34 mg **CHOL**; 871 mg **SODIUM**; 44 g **CARB**; 4 g **FIBER**; 19 g **PRO**

Beef-Sweet Pepper Calzones

Make and bake a double batch of these pocket sandwiches and freeze some or all for future meals. Cool completely, then wrap each one individually in plastic wrap and freeze in a tightly sealed freezer bag. To reheat, unwrap and warm in 1-minute bursts in the microwave (2 to 3 minutes total).

MAKES 4 servings   **PREP** 30 minutes   **BAKE** 12 minutes   **STAND** 5 minutes

8	ounces extra-lean ground beef
⅓	cup chopped red sweet pepper
⅓	cup chopped green sweet pepper
¼	teaspoon dried Italian seasoning, crushed
¼	teaspoon dried oregano, crushed
	Nonstick cooking spray
1	13.8-ounce can refrigerated pizza dough
¾	cup shredded mozzarella cheese (3 ounces)
1	cup reduced-sodium tomato-base pasta sauce, warmed

1 For the filling, in a large nonstick skillet cook meat over medium heat until browned. Drain off fat. Add sweet peppers, Italian seasoning, and oregano to meat in skillet; cook over medium heat 3 minutes or until sweet peppers are tender.

2 Preheat oven to 450°F. Line a large baking sheet with foil; lightly coat foil with cooking spray. On a lightly floured surface, gently shape pizza dough into a 12-inch square, using a rolling pin as needed. Cut dough into four 6-inch squares. Place some filling in the center of each square. Sprinkle with ½ cup of the cheese.

3 For each calzone, lift a corner of the dough and stretch over filling to opposite corner to make a triangle. Press edges with the tines of a fork to seal. Place on prepared baking sheet.

4 Bake 12 to 14 minutes or until lightly browned. Sprinkle with remaining cheese. Let stand 5 minutes. Serve with warmed pasta sauce.

PER SERVING 431 **CAL**; 12 g **FAT** (4 g **SAT**); 49 mg **CHOL**; 852 mg **SODIUM**; 53 g **CARB**; 3 g **FIBER**; 27 g **PRO**

Chicken-Spinach Calzones

Prepared ingredients such as rotisserie chicken, jarred pizza sauce, and refrigerated pizza dough make these kid-friendly calzones a snap to make.

MAKES 8 servings   **PREP** 30 minutes   **BAKE** 18 minutes

- **3   cups chopped rotisserie chicken**
- **2½ cups chopped fresh spinach**
- **1½ cups shredded pizza cheese (6 ounces)**
- **1   14- to 15-ounce jar pizza sauce**
- **2   13.8-ounce packages refrigerated pizza dough**
  Milk
  Finely shredded Parmesan or Romano cheese (optional)

1 Preheat oven to 375°F. For the filling, in a large bowl combine chicken, spinach, and pizza cheese. Stir in ½ cup of the pizza sauce.

2 On a lightly floured surface, roll one package of the pizza dough to a 12-inch square. Cut into four 6-inch squares.

3 For each calzone, place about ⅔ cup filling onto half of each dough square, about ½ inch from edge. Moisten edges with water and fold over, forming a triangle or rectangle. Pinch or press with a fork to seal edges. Using the tip of a knife, cut small slits in tops of each; place on an ungreased baking sheet. Repeat Steps 2 and 3 with second package of pizza dough.

4 Brush tops of calzones with milk and, if desired, sprinkle with Parmesan cheese. Bake 18 minutes or until calzones are golden brown and heated through. In a small saucepan heat the remaining pizza sauce; serve with calzones.

PER SERVING 295 **CAL**; 9 g **FAT** (3 g **SAT**); 35 mg **CHOL**; 1,221 mg **SODIUM**; 31 g **CARB**; 1 g **FIBER**; 22 g **PRO**

Sausage and Spinach Skillet Pizza

Baking this hearty pie in a cast-iron skillet results in an extra-crisp crust.

MAKES 6 servings **PREP** 35 minutes **BAKE** 15 minutes **STAND** 5 minutes

1	15-ounce can tomato sauce
3	tablespoons grated Parmesan cheese
2	tablespoons tomato paste
¾	teaspoon dried oregano, crushed
½	teaspoon dried basil, crushed
⅛	teaspoon crushed red pepper
1	5- to 6-ounce package fresh baby spinach
2	teaspoons water
	Olive oil
1	pound frozen pizza or bread dough, thawed
8	ounces bulk Italian sausage, cooked and drained
1½	to 2 cups shredded mozzarella cheese
	Crushed red pepper (optional)

1 Preheat oven to 475°F. In a small bowl combine tomato sauce, 2 tablespoons of the Parmesan cheese, the tomato paste, oregano, basil, and the ⅛ teaspoon crushed red pepper. Set aside.

2 Place spinach in a large microwave-safe bowl; sprinkle with the water. Cover with a microwave-safe plate. Heat on high 30 seconds. Continue cooking in 10-second intervals just until spinach is wilted. Let stand 2 minutes; carefully remove plate. Transfer spinach to a sieve; press out excess liquid.

3 Brush a 12-inch cast-iron or other heavy oven-going skillet with oil. On a lightly floured surface, roll pizza dough into a 14-inch circle. Transfer to prepared skillet. Roll edges to form a rim. Brush dough lightly with oil. Spread tomato sauce mixture on dough; top with sausage and spinach. Sprinkle with mozzarella cheese and the remaining Parmesan cheese.

4 Cook pizza in skillet over medium-high heat 3 minutes. Place skillet in oven. Bake 15 to 20 minutes or until crust and cheeses are lightly browned. Let stand 5 minutes before serving. Using a spatula, slide pizza out of skillet. Cut into wedges. If desired, sprinkle with additional crushed red pepper.

PER SERVING 449 **CAL**; 23 g **FAT** (9 g **SAT**); 53 mg **CHOL**;
1,237 mg **SODIUM**; 40 g **CARB**; 3 g **FIBER**; 19 g **PRO**

MEAT AND POTATO PIZZA

Meat and Potato Pizza

Putting potatoes on pizza may sound odd, but Italians do it all the time. Rosemary-garlic butter brushed on the crust before layering on the ingredients gives this pizza fabulous flavor.

MAKES 4 servings **PREP** 20 minutes **BAKE** 14 minutes

3	**tablespoons butter, softened**
4	**cloves garlic, minced**
1	**teaspoon snipped fresh rosemary**
1	**13.8-ounce package refrigerated pizza dough**
2	**russet potatoes, peeled and very thinly sliced***
7	**ounces cooked smoked sausage, thinly sliced**
5	**slices bacon, crisp-cooked and crumbled**
1	**cup shredded mozzarella cheese**

1 Preheat oven to 425°F. In a small bowl combine butter, garlic, and rosemary.

2 In a 15×10×1-inch baking pan, unroll pizza dough. Press to a 14×10-inch rectangle. Pinch edges to form a rim. Spread butter mixture on the dough. Top with potatoes, sausage, bacon, and cheese.

3 Bake 14 to 16 minutes or until crust is golden brown and potatoes are tender. Let stand several minutes before slicing.

*Tip For the potatoes to cook thoroughly on the pizza they have to be very thinly and uniformly sliced. Use a mandolin, food processor, or very sharp knife.

PER SERVING 669 **CAL**; 36 g **FAT** (16 g **SAT**); 78 mg **CHOL**; 1,661 mg **SODIUM**; 62 g **CARB**; 3 g **FIBER**; 26 g **PRO**

Steak, Egg, and Goat Cheese Pizza

This steak-and-egg pizza makes a fine supper or a fun brunch dish.

MAKES 6 servings **PREP** 25 minutes **BAKE** 24 minutes

	Nonstick cooking spray
1	**13.8-ounce package refrigerated pizza dough with whole grain**
3	**to 4 ounces thinly sliced cooked roast beef**
	Olive oil
3	**cloves garlic, thinly sliced**
1½	**cups shredded mozzarella cheese**
½	**cup torn fresh kale**
¼	**cup bottled roasted red sweet peppers strips**
2	**ounces goat cheese (chèvre), crumbled**
6	**eggs**
	Dash black pepper
1	**tablespoon snipped fresh chives**

1 Preheat oven to 400°. On a large lightly greased baking sheet, stretch pizza dough to a 15×12-inch rectangle. Bake 6 minutes. Remove from oven and let cool slightly. (Crust will just be set and not brown.) Meanwhile, cut roast beef slices into strips; set aside.

2 Brush crust with olive oil and sprinkle with garlic. Top with roast beef, mozzarella, kale, and roasted peppers. Crumble goat cheese over pizza. Carefully crack the eggs directly on the pizza, about 1 to 2 inches apart. Season eggs with pepper.

3 Bake 18 minutes or until crust is golden brown, egg whites are completely set, and egg yolks begin to thicken. Sprinkle with chives before serving.

PER SERVING 413 **CAL**; 20 g **FAT** (9 g **SAT**); 223 mg **CHOL**; 857 mg **SODIUM**; 33 g **CARB**; 2 g **FIBER**; 23 g **PRO**

Chicken, Asparagus, and Mushroom Flatbreads

The crust for these spring-inspired flatbreads is not yeasted but rather made more like a pastry—by cutting shortening into flour. The result is a thin, delightfully crackly crust.

MAKES 6 servings   **PREP** 30 minutes   **BAKE** 16 minutes

1	tablespoon cornmeal
2	cups all-purpose flour
½	teaspoon salt
½	teaspoon baking powder
½	teaspoon black pepper
⅓	cup shortening
¾	cup cold water
3	tablespoons olive oil
1	cup stemmed and sliced fresh shiitake mushrooms
1	small red onion, thinly sliced
6	ounces thin fresh asparagus spears, trimmed and cut into 2-inch pieces (about 1 cup)
1	cup shredded rotisserie chicken
3	tablespoons snipped fresh Italian parsley
1	tablespoon Dijon mustard
1	teaspoon snipped fresh thyme
1½	cups shredded mozzarella and/or Swiss cheese (6 ounces)

1 Preheat oven to 500°F. Line a large baking sheet with foil. Sprinkle foil with cornmeal; set aside. In a medium bowl combine flour, salt, baking powder, and pepper. Using a pasty blender, cut shortening into flour mixture until the mixture resembles coarse crumbs. Make a well in the center of the mixture. Add the water and stir with a fork until combined. Knead dough a few times until smooth.

2 Divide dough in half. On a lightly floured surface, roll each dough portion into a 14×5-inch oval. Arrange dough ovals on the prepared baking sheet. Brush with 1 tablespoon oil. Bake 11 to 13 minutes or until lightly golden brown.

3 Meanwhile, for topping, in a large skillet heat the remaining 2 tablespoons oil over medium-high heat. Add mushrooms and onion; cook and stir 3 minutes. Add asparagus; cook 3 minutes more or just until tender. Remove from heat. Stir in chicken, parsley, mustard, and thyme.

4 Spoon half the topping over each crust. Sprinkle with cheese. Bake 5 minutes more or until cheese is melted. Slice each flatbread into thirds.

PER SERVING 435 **CAL**; 24 g **FAT** (7 g **SAT**); 39 mg **CHOL**; 551 mg **SODIUM**; 36 g **CARB**; 2 g **FIBER**; 18 g **PRO**

Spicy Fish and Chips

This oven-baked version of a classic English pub dish features crisp-coated fish and sweet potato "chips" that offer great taste and good nutrition.

MAKES 4 servings **PREP** 15 minutes **BAKE** 20 minutes

- **1** **pound fresh or frozen white-flesh fish fillets, such as cod or tilapia, about ½ inch thick**
  Nonstick olive oil cooking spray
- **1** **pound sweet potatoes, cut into ¼-inch slices**
- **1** **tablespoon olive oil**
- **1** **teaspoon Old Bay seasoning or seafood seasoning**
- **2½** **teaspoons chili powder**
- **¾** **teaspoon salt**
- **1** **egg, lightly beaten**
- **⅓** **cup all-purpose flour**
- **⅓** **cup fine dry bread crumbs**
- **1** **teaspoon paprika**
- **¼** **teaspoon black pepper**
  Lemon wedges (optional)
  Snipped fresh parsley (optional)

1 Thaw fish, if frozen. Cut fish into 3×2-inch pieces. Rinse fish with cold water; pat dry with paper towels. Cover and chill until needed.

2 Preheat oven to 425°F. Line an extra-large baking sheet with foil; lightly coat with cooking spray; set aside.

3 For chips, pat sweet potatoes dry with paper towels; place in a large bowl. Add oil, Old Bay seasoning, ½ teaspoon of the chili powder, and ½ teaspoon of the salt. Toss to coat. Arrange potatoes in a single layer on half the prepared baking sheet. Bake 10 minutes.

4 Meanwhile, for fish, place egg in a shallow dish. Place flour in another shallow dish. In a third shallow dish combine bread crumbs, the remaining chili powder, the paprika, the remaining salt, and the pepper. Coat fish pieces with flour. Dip in egg, then in bread crumb mixture. Generously coat crumbs with cooking spray.

5 Remove baking sheet from oven. Using a spatula, carefully turn potatoes over. Place fish on the opposite half of hot baking sheet; return to oven. Bake 10 to 15 minutes more or until potatoes are golden brown and fish flakes easily when tested with a fork. If desired, serve with lemon wedges and sprinkle with parsley.

PER SERVING 319 **CAL**; 6 g **FAT** (1 g **SAT**); 95 mg **CHOL**; 838 mg **SODIUM**; 39 g **CARB**; 5 g **FIBER**; 26 g **PRO**

CHAPTER 9
sweet
endings

The perfect dessert makes even the simplest occasion special.

PEANUT BUTTER FINGERS

CAKES

Blueberry Buckle with Zippy Lime-Ginger Glaze, 173

Highlander Heaven Cake, 167

Key Lime Coconut Cake with Marshmallow
Frosting, 169

Marbleous Chocolate-Peanut Butter Cake with Salted
Caramel Glaze, 170

Shortcut German-Chocolate Cake, 168

DESSERTS

Cherry-Orange Clafouti, 174

Cider-Baked Stuffed Apples with Salty
Caramel Sauce, 184

Double-Chocolate Bread Pudding with
Strawberry Sauce, 186

Root Beer Float Ice Cream Sandwiches, 179

Spiced Pear-Cranberry Cobbler, 185

COOKIES AND BROWNIES

Cast-Iron Hot Gingerbread Cookie, 175

Frosted Zucchini Brownies, 178

Peanut Butter Fingers, 177

PIES AND TARTS

Buttermilk Pie, 180

Claret Poached Pear Sour Cream Tart, 183

Highlander Heaven Cake

When Corrie King switched from the night shift to the day shift at the Wisconsin care facility where she works as a nurse, she went from drinking coffee all night to craving a sweet treat made with coffee during the day. Highlander Grogg Coffee from the Door County Coffee & Tea Company is a favorite, and she created this coffee-flavor cake topped with butterscotch-coffee frosting as an entry into their 2014 recipe contest. The first-place prize was a year's worth of coffee—which just ran out, she says.

MAKES 12 servings   **PREP** 20 minutes   **BAKE** 30 minutes   **COOL** 2 hours

1	package 2-layer-size white cake mix
1	cup double-strength brewed Door County Highlander Grogg Coffee*, cooled
3	eggs
⅓	cup vegetable oil
½	cup butter, softened
⅓	cup butterscotch-flavor ice cream topping
1	teaspoon vanilla
⅛	teaspoon salt
1	pound powdered sugar (about 4 cups)
2	to 4 tablespoons double-strength brewed Door County Highlander Grogg Coffee,* cooled

1 Preheat oven to 350°F. Grease a 13×9-inch baking pan. In a large bowl combine the cake mix, 1 cup brewed Highlander Grogg, eggs, and oil. Beat with a mixer on low just until combined. Beat on medium for 2 minutes. Spread batter into the prepared pan.

2 Bake 30 to 35 minutes or until a wooden toothpick inserted near center comes out clean. Cool completely in pan on a wire rack.

3 For the frosting, in a large bowl beat butter, butterscotch topping, vanilla, and salt with a mixer on medium until fluffy. Gradually beat in about half the powdered sugar. Add the 2 tablespoons of the Highlander Grogg. Gradually beat in remaining powdered sugar and enough remaining Grogg to reach spreading consistency. Spread frosting over cooled cake.

*Tip To brew double-strength coffee, use the same amount of coffee grounds you typically would use and half the amount of water.

PER SERVING 477 **CAL**; 17 g **FAT** (7 g **SAT**); 67 mg **CHOL**; 430 mg **SODIUM**; 80 g **CARB**; 3 g **PRO**

Shortcut German-Chocolate Cake

A jar of caramel ice cream topping stirred together with toasted coconut and pecans stands in for the cooked topping in traditional German chocolate cake.

MAKES 8 servings　**PREP** 30 minutes　**BAKE** 36 minutes　**COOL** 10 minutes

1½ **cups broken pecans**
¾ **cup sugar**
⅓ **cup coarsely chopped sweet baking chocolate**
¼ **cup Dutch processed or unsweetened cocoa powder**
1 **teaspoon baking powder**
¼ **teaspoon baking soda**
5 **eggs**
1½ **teaspoons vanilla**
1 **recipe Toasted Coconut-Pecan Caramel Sauce**

1 Preheat oven to 350°F. Grease a 9×1½-inch round cake pan; line bottom with parchment paper. Grease parchment paper; set pan aside.

2 For cake, in a food processor combine pecans, sugar, chopped chocolate, cocoa powder, baking powder, and baking soda, pulsing until nuts are ground. Add eggs and vanilla. Process until nearly smooth. Spread batter in prepared pan. Bake 30 minutes or until a toothpick inserted near center of cake comes out clean.

3 Remove from oven. Cool in pan on wire rack 10 minutes. Remove cake from pan; cool completely on wire rack.

4 Cut into wedges and place on dessert plates. Spoon Toasted Coconut-Pecan Caramel Sauce on cake.

Toasted Coconut-Pecan Caramel Sauce Preheat oven to 350°F. Spread ½ cup flaked coconut and ½ cup pecans in a thin layer in a shallow baking pan. Bake 6 to 8 minutes or until the coconut is toasted and the nuts are golden brown, stirring once or twice. In a medium bowl stir together one 12.25-ounce jar caramel ice cream topping and toasted coconut and pecans. Serve immediately or warm slightly in microwave before serving. Makes about 1½ cups.

PER SERVING 526 **CAL**; 28 g **FAT** (5 g **SAT**); 133 mg **CHOL**; 269 mg **SODIUM**; 63 g **CARB**; 4 g **FIBER**; 8 g **PRO**

Key Lime Coconut Cake with Marshmallow Frosting

Frost this cake right before serving if possible for the creamiest, smoothest and fluffiest frosting. The sugar in the frosting starts to crystallize as it sits.

MAKES 12 servings **PREP** 45 minutes **BAKE** 40 minutes **COOL** 15 minutes

¾   **cup butter, softened**
3   **eggs**
2½   **teaspoons baking powder**
½   **teaspoon salt**
1½   **cups sugar**
1   **teaspoon vanilla**
½   **cup milk**
½   **cup cream of coconut***
1   **tablespoon Key lime or Persian lime zest**
¼   **cup Key lime or Persian lime juice**
2½   **cups all-purpose flour**
1   **recipe Marshmallow Frosting**
½   **cup raw coconut chips or flaked coconut, lightly toasted (tip, page 31)**
    Thinly sliced Key lime or Persian lime

1 Let butter and eggs stand at room temperature 30 minutes. Grease and flour a 10-inch tube pan. Preheat oven to 350°.

2 In a large mixing bowl beat butter, baking powder, and salt with a mixer on medium 30 seconds. Gradually add sugar, about ¼ cup at a time, until well combined. Scrape sides of bowl; beat 2 minutes more. Add eggs one at a time, beating well after each addition. Beat in vanilla. In a small bowl combine milk, cream of coconut, lime zest, and lime juice. Alternately add flour and milk mixture to butter mixture, beating on low after each addition just until combined. Spoon batter evenly into the prepared pan.

3 Bake 40 minutes or until a wooden toothpick inserted near center comes out clean. Cool cake in pan on a wire rack for 15 minutes. Remove cake from pan; cool on wire rack.

4 Place cooled cake on a serving plate. Generously frost with Marshmallow Frosting. Sprinkle with coconut chips and lime slices. Preferably serve cake soon after frosting.

Marshmallow Frosting In the top of a double boiler combine 1½ cups sugar, ⅓ cup cold water, 2 egg whites, and ¼ teaspoon cream of tartar. Beat with an electric mixer on low 30 seconds. Place over boiling water (upper pan should not touch water). Cook, beating constantly with mixer on high, about 10 minutes or until frosting forms stiff peaks (tips stand straight) and an instant-read thermometer inserted in mixture registers 145°F for 3 minutes or 160°F for 15 seconds. Scrape pan occasionally. Remove pan from heat. Add 1 teaspoon vanilla. Beat 2 to 3 minutes more or until frosting reaches spreading consistency.

***Tip** Before measuring, stir the cream of coconut in the can.

PER SERVING 471 **CAL**; 18 g **FAT** (12 g **SAT**); 78 mg **CHOL**; 334 mg **SODIUM**; 73 g **CARB**; 1 g **FIBER**; 6 g **PRO**

Marbleous Chocolate-Peanut Butter Cake with Salted Caramel Glaze

Use a large-flaked sea salt—such as Maldon from England—to sprinkle on this decadent cake.

MAKES 12 servings **PREP** 30 minutes **BAKE** 40 minutes **COOL** 1 hour

2   **eggs**
2   **cups all-purpose flour**
4   **teaspoons baking powder**
½   **teaspoon baking soda**
¼   **teaspoon salt**
⅛   **teaspoon ground cinnamon**
½   **cup unsalted butter, softened**
1¼   **cups sugar**
¾   **cup sour cream**
1   **teaspoon vanilla**
⅓   **cup milk**
3   **ounces bittersweet chocolate, melted and cooled**
½   **cup creamy peanut butter**
1   **recipe Salted Caramel Glaze**
     Chopped peanuts (optional)
     Sea salt (optional)

1 Let eggs stand at room temperature 30 minutes. Grease a 10-inch fluted tube pan. Stir together the flour, baking powder, baking soda, salt, and cinnamon.

2 Preheat oven to 350°F. In a large bowl beat butter with a mixer on medium 30 seconds. Gradually add sugar, about ¼ cup at a time, beating on medium until combined. Scrape bowl; beat 2 minutes more. Add eggs, one at a time, beating well after each addition. Beat in sour cream and vanilla. Alternately add flour mixture and milk, beating on low after each addition just until combined.

3 Transfer half the batter to a medium bowl; stir in melted chocolate. Stir peanut butter into the remaining batter.

4 Alternately drop spoonfuls of chocolate and peanut butter batters into prepared pan. Using a small metal spatula, swirl batters slightly to marble (do not overmix).

5 Bake 40 to 45 minutes or until a toothpick comes out clean. Cool cake in pan 15 minutes. Remove cake from pan; cool completely on wire rack. Transfer to a serving plate. Drizzle cake with half the Salted Caramel Glaze. If desired, sprinkle with chopped peanuts and sea salt. Pass the remaining glaze.

Salted Caramel Glaze In a small heavy saucepan melt ¼ cup unsalted butter over medium-low heat. Stir in ¼ cup packed brown sugar and ¼ cup granulated sugar. Bring to boiling, stirring constantly. Stir in ½ cup heavy cream and return to boiling. Boil 2 minutes, stirring constantly. Remove from heat; stir in ½ to ¾ teaspoon sea salt. Cool completely.

PER SERVING 466 **CAL**; 27 g **FAT** (14 g **SAT**); 86 mg **CHOL**; 369 mg **SODIUM**; 53 g **CARB**; 2 g **FIBER**; 7 g **PRO**

Blueberry Buckle with Zippy Lime-Ginger Glaze

Although there's some confusion about the differences among cobblers, crisps, "slumps," and buckles, a buckle is defined as a fruited cake topped by a streusel that makes the top look "buckled." This moist, chock-full-of-blueberries buckle with a "zippy" lime-ginger glaze took top prize at the 2015 North Carolina Blueberry Festival Recipe Contest in Burgaw, North Carolina. The only contest stipulation was the recipe should be original and contain at least 1 cup of fresh North Carolina blueberries.

MAKES 9 servings **PREP** 30 minutes **BAKE** 45 minutes **COOK** 5 minutes

- 1⅔ cups all-purpose flour
- 1 teaspoon baking powder
- ½ teaspoon salt
- ¼ teaspoon baking soda
- ¼ teaspoon nutmeg
- ½ cup all-purpose flour
- ⅓ cup sugar
- ⅛ teaspoon salt
- 2 teaspoons lime zest
- ¼ cup unsalted butter, chilled
- 6 tablespoons unsalted butter, softened
- ¾ cup sugar
- 2 teaspoons lemon zest
- 2 eggs
- ½ cup buttermilk
- 2 cups North Carolina blueberries
- ⅓ cup sugar
- ¼ cup fresh lime juice
- 1 tablespoon grated fresh ginger
- Plain yogurt, crème fraîche, or whipped cream (optional)

1 Preheat oven to 350°F. Grease an 8×8×2-inch baking pan; set aside. In a medium bowl combine the 1⅔ cups flour, the baking powder, ½ teaspoon salt, baking soda, and nutmeg.

2 For the crumb topping, in a small bowl combine ½ cup flour, ⅓ cup sugar, ⅛ teaspoon salt, and lime zest. Using a pastry blender, cut in ¼ cup chilled butter until pea size. Chill until ready to use.

3 In a medium mixing bowl beat 6 tablespoons softened butter with a mixer on medium 30 seconds. Add the ¾ cup sugar and lemon zest. Beat on medium to high 3 to 5 minutes or until light and fluffy. Add eggs one at a time, beating well after each addition. Alternately add flour mixture and buttermilk to beaten egg mixture; beating on low after each addition just until combined. Gently fold in 1 cup blueberries.

4 Spread batter in prepared pan. Sprinkle with remaining blueberries. Sprinkle chilled crumb topping over blueberries.

5 Meanwhile, for the glaze when the cake is almost done baking, in a small saucepan combine ⅓ cup sugar, lime juice, and ginger. Cook over medium-low heat 5 to 7 minutes or until syrupy, stirring occasionally.

6 Bake 45 to 50 minutes or until golden. Immediately pour hot glaze over the hot cake.

7 Serve cake warm with yogurt, crème fraîche, or whipped cream, if desired.

PER SERVING 389 **CAL**; 14 g **FAT** (9 g **SAT**); 76 mg **CHOL**; 284 mg **SODIUM**; 61 g **CARB**; 2 g **FIBER**; 5 g **PRO**

Cherry-Orange Clafouti

Clafouti is a homey country-French dessert that walks the line between being a pudding and a cake. Cherries are the most traditional fruit for clafouti, but plums, peaches, or pears can be used as well.

MAKES 6 servings **PREP** 25 minutes **BAKE** 35 minutes

1	tablespoon butter, softened
3	eggs
½	cup granulated sugar
¾	cup whole milk
½	cup whipping cream
½	cup all-purpose flour
2	tablespoons orange juice
2	teaspoons orange zest
1	teaspoon almond extract
¼	teaspoon salt
3	cups fresh or frozen* pitted sweet cherries
	Powdered sugar
	Crème fraîche or soft whipped cream

1 Preheat oven to 375°. Butter a 10-inch oven-going skillet or six 6- to 8-ounce ramekins with the softened butter; set aside. In a blender combine eggs, granulated sugar, milk, cream, flour, orange juice, orange zest, almond extract, and salt. Blend until smooth.

2 Arrange cherries in the prepared skillet. Carefully pour batter over berries. Bake 10 minutes. Reduce oven temperature to 350°F. Bake 25 to 30 minutes (20 to 25 minutes more for ramekins) or until filling is set and top is golden brown.

3 Sprinkle with powdered sugar and serve warm with crème fraîche.

*Arrange frozen cherries on a baking sheet lined with paper towels. Thaw 10 to 15 minutes (berries will not be fully thawed). Transfer to skillet, trying not to break cherries.

PER SERVING 349 **CAL**; 18 g **FAT** (11 g **SAT**); 149 mg **CHOL**; 174 mg **SODIUM**; 41 g **CARB**; 2 g **FIBER**; 6 g **PRO**

Cast-Iron Hot Gingerbread Cookie

For another way to serve this sweet and spicy dessert, substitute the pineapple for blueberries, briefly cooked, and the caramel ice cream topping for lemon curd.

MAKES 4 servings **PREP** 25 minutes **GRILL** 15 minutes

1	**tablespoon butter, softened**
1	**cup all-purpose flour**
1	**teaspoon ground ginger**
½	**teaspoon baking soda**
¼	**teaspoon ground cinnamon**
¼	**teaspoon ground cloves**
	Dash salt
⅓	**cup shortening**
½	**cup sugar**
1	**egg**
2	**tablespoons molasses**
4	**slices fresh pineapple**
1	**tablespoon butter**
	Caramel ice cream topping (optional)
	Cinnamon or butter pecan ice cream

1 Preheat oven to 350°F. Using the softened butter, generously butter a 7- to 8-inch cast-iron skillet or two 5-inch cast-iron skillets. In a medium bowl stir together flour, ginger, baking soda, cinnamon, cloves, and salt.

2 In another bowl beat shortening with a mixer on low 30 seconds. Add sugar; beat until combined. Beat in egg and molasses until combined. Beat in as much of the flour mixture as you can. Stir in any remaining flour mixture. Pour into the prepared skillet(s), spreading evenly. Bake about 18 minutes for large skillet or 12 to 14 minutes for small skillets, or until edges are set.

3 Meanwhile, in another large skillet cook pineapple slices in 1 tablespoon hot butter over medium-high heat 4 to 5 minutes or until golden brown, turning once.

4 Cool cookie(s) slightly (center will fall slightly). If desired, cut up pineapple. Top gingerbread cookie(s) with pineapple and, if desired, drizzle with ice cream topping. Serve with ice cream.

Grilling Directions Prepare as directed through Step 2, except do not preheat oven. Prepare grill for indirect heat. Place skillet(s) on grill rack over indirect medium heat. Grill, covered, until edges of cookie are set. Allow 15 to 18 minutes for a large skillet or 10 to 12 minutes for small skillets. The last 5 to 10 minutes of grilling, add pineapple slices to grill over direct heat. Grill, covered, until golden brown, turning once.

*Tip For eight servings, double the recipe and use two 7- to 8-inch cast-iron skillets.

PER SERVING 624 **CAL**; 31 g **FAT** (11 g **SAT**); 81 mg **CHOL**; 348 mg **SODIUM**; 82 g **CARB**; 2 g **FIBER**; 7 g **PRO**

Peanut Butter Fingers

A classic flavor combination takes yet another form in these quick-to-fix treats. Warm peanut butter bars are topped with chocolate pieces until melted, then drizzled with peanut butter icing.

MAKES 32 servings **PREP** 15 minutes **BAKE** 15 minutes **STAND** 5 minutes

½   **cup butter, softened**
½   **cup granulated sugar**
½   **cup packed brown sugar**
1   **egg**
⅓   **cup peanut butter**
½   **teaspoon baking soda**
½   **teaspoon vanilla**
    Dash salt
1   **cup all-purpose flour**
1   **cup rolled oats**
1½ **cups semisweet chocolate pieces**
⅓   **cup sifted powdered sugar**
3   **tablespoons peanut butter**
2   **to 3 tablespoons milk**

1 Preheat oven to 350°F. Grease a 13×9×2-inch baking pan. In a medium bowl beat butter with a mixer on medium to high 30 seconds. Add granulated and brown sugars. Beat until thoroughly combined.

2 Add egg, the ⅓ cup peanut butter, the baking soda, vanilla, and salt. Beat until thoroughly combined. Stir in flour and oats. Spread into prepared pan.

3 Bake 15 to 18 minutes or until edges are light brown.

4 Sprinkle with chocolate pieces; let stand 5 minutes to soften.

5 Meanwhile, for icing, in a bowl stir together powdered sugar, the 3 tablespoons peanut butter, and milk, 1 tablespoon at a time, to reach drizzling consistency.

6 Spread softened chocolate over bars. Drizzle with icing. Cool in the pan on a wire rack before cutting into bars.

PER SERVING 145 **CAL**; 8 g **FAT** (3 g **SAT**); 14 mg **CHOL**; 73 mg **SODIUM**; 18 g **CARB**; 1 g **FIBER**; 2 g **PRO**

Frosted Zucchini Brownies

These moist brownies offer a sweet way to use up some of the bounty of the most prolific plant in the vegetable garden.

MAKES 50 servings **PREP** 20 minutes **BAKE** 30 minutes

- 1½ **cups all-purpose flour**
- 1 **teaspoon baking soda**
- ¾ **teaspoon baking powder**
- ½ **teaspoon salt**
- 2 **eggs**
- 1½ **cups sugar**
- ¾ **cup vegetable oil**
- 2 **ounces unsweetened chocolate, melted and cooled**
- 1½ **cups finely shredded zucchini**
- ½ **cup finely chopped nuts**
- 6 **ounces cream cheese**
- 6 **tablespoons butter**
- 1½ **teaspoons vanilla**
- 3½ **to 4 cups powdered sugar**

1 Preheat oven to 350°F. For brownies, in a small bowl combine flour, baking soda, baking powder, and salt.

2 In a large mixing bowl beat eggs with a mixer on low until combined. Add sugar, oil, and melted chocolate; beat until blended. With mixer on low add flour mixture. Beat just until well combined. With a spoon, stir in zucchini and nuts. Turn batter into a greased and floured 15×10×1-inch baking pan.

3 Bake 30 to 35 minutes or until surface springs back when pressed lightly. Cool in pan on wire rack.

4 Meanwhile, for cream cheese frosting, in a large mixing bowl beat cream cheese, butter, and vanilla with a mixer on medium until light and fluffy. Gradually beat in powdered sugar to reach spreading consistency. Spread over cooled brownies in pan.

PER SERVING 140 **CAL**; 7 g **FAT** (2 g **SAT**); 15 mg **CHOL**; 83 mg **SODIUM**; 18 g **CARB**; 1 g **PRO**

Root Beer Float Ice Cream Sandwiches

These cold and creamy treats—a perfect dessert to serve at a backyard summer barbecue—can be made and stored in the freezer up to 1 month.

MAKES 14 servings **PREP** 30 minutes **BAKE** 12 minutes **FREEZE** 1 hour

1	**cup butter, softened**
1	**cup sugar**
1½	**teaspoons baking powder**
½	**teaspoon salt**
2	**egg yolks**
¼	**teaspoon root beer flavoring**
2	**cups all-purpose flour**
½	**cup crushed root beer-flavor hard candies (about 12)**
¼	**cup sugar**
1	**1.75-quart container vanilla ice cream**

1 Preheat oven to 325°. Line baking sheets with parchment paper. In a large mixing bowl beat butter with a mixer on medium to high 30 seconds. Add 1 cup sugar, the baking powder, and salt. Beat until combined, scraping sides of bowl occasionally. Beat in egg yolks and root beer flavoring. Beat in as much of the flour as you can with the mixer. Stir in any remaining flour and the crushed root beer-flavor hard candies.

2 Shape dough into twenty-eight 1½-inch balls. Roll in ¼ cup sugar to coat. Place balls 2 inches apart on prepared baking sheets.

3 Bake 12 to 14 minutes or until edges are set; do not let edges brown. Cool cookies on baking sheet 2 minutes. Transfer cookies to a wire rack and let cool.

4 To assemble sandwiches, allow ice cream to soften slightly. For each ice cream sandwich, press about ½ cup ice cream between two cookies. Individually wrap each ice cream sandwich in plastic wrap. Freeze 1 hour or until firm. Store in freezer up to 1 month. Let stand at room temperature 5 minutes before serving.

PER SERVING 552 **CAL**; 31 g **FAT** (20 g **SAT**); 160 mg **CHOL**; 318 mg **SODIUM**; 62 g **CARB**; 6 g **PRO**

Buttermilk Pie

This old-fashioned favorite was a specialty of Patty Hummel's grandmother, who told her it was a "Depression" pie. "If you had fruit trees, the fruit was sold to make money," Patty says. "If any fruit was to be used for pie, it was for Sunday dinner." Everyone had cows, so buttermilk pie was an everyday pie. With this creamy pie, Patty, the librarian at the Allison, Iowa, public library took top prize in the Tone's "Everyday Family Recipe" Contest held at the 2015 Iowa State Fair.

MAKES 8 servings **PREP** 20 minutes **BAKE** 45 minutes

½ **cup butter or margarine, softened**
1¾ **cups sugar**
3 **eggs**
3 **tablespoons all-purpose flour**
½ **teaspoon Tone's Clear Vanilla**
½ **teaspoon Tone's Imitation Butter Flavor**
¼ **teaspoon Tone's Pure Almond Extract**
   Dash salt
1 **cup buttermilk**
1 **purchased 9-inch unbaked deep dish piecrust or homemade piecrust**

1 Preheat oven to 350°F. In a medium bowl beat butter with a mixer on medium to high 30 seconds. Add sugar and beat on medium speed 2 minutes. Add eggs and beat 1 minute or until creamy. Add flour, extracts, and salt; beat 1 to 2 minutes or until well combined. While the mixer is running, very slowly add the buttermilk in a thin stream. (This creates the smooth and creamy texture.) Continue to beat on medium until all buttermilk is incorporated. Pour filling into piecrust.

2 Place the pie on the center rack in the oven. Bake 45 to 50 minutes or until a knife inserted in center comes out clean and top is golden. (Center of pie will jiggle slightly.) Cool completely on a wire rack.

PER SERVING 453 **CAL**; 21 g **FAT** (11 g **SAT**); 102 mg **CHOL**; 291 mg **SODIUM**; 63 g **CARB**; 1 g **FIBER**; 5 g **PRO**

Claret Poached Pear Sour Cream Tart

R'becca Groff of Cedar Rapids, Iowa, says she "ruined a lot of wine figuring out the glaze" for this elegant fruit tart that captured first place in the Iowa Egg Council's 2015 Decadent Dessert Contest. The contest specifies only that no fewer than four eggs be used. It was worth the effort. With the $750 in prize money, R'becca bought a new glider for the house she and her husband recently built.

MAKES 8 servings **PREP** 25 minutes **COOK** 25 minutes **BAKE** 15 minutes + 1 hour

4	winter pears (such as Bosc, Comice, or Highland)
2	cups claret wine
2	cups water
1	cup sugar
3	whole cloves
3	inches stick cinnamon
1	slice fresh lemon
1	tablespoon cornstarch
¼	cup cold water
1¼	cups all-purpose flour
½	cup butter, softened
2	tablespoons sour cream
¾	cup sugar
¼	cup all-purpose flour
4	egg yolks
1	cup sour cream
1	teaspoon vanilla
	Finely shredded peel of 1 lemon (2 teaspoons)

1 Peel, halve, and core pears. In a large saucepan combine wine, the 2 cups water, 1 cup sugar, cloves, cinnamon, and lemon slice. Add pears. Simmer, covered, 15 to 20 minutes or until pears are tender. Remove pears from poaching liquid; let stand until cool enough to handle.

2 For the glaze, strain poaching liquid to remove cloves and cinnamon; return 1 cup to the saucepan and return to medium heat. In a small bowl combine cornstarch and ¼ cup water until smooth. Gradually whisk cornstarch mixture into heated poaching liquid. Cook and stir until thickened and bubbly; cook 1 more minute. Pour glaze into a bowl and chill until ready to serve.

3 Preheat oven to 375°F. In a bowl beat 1¼ cups flour, butter, and 2 tablespoons sour cream with a mixer on medium until dough clings together. Pat dough into the bottom and up the sides of an ungreased 10-inch tart pan or gratin dish. Bake 15 minutes or until crust is set, dry, and edges are lightly browned. Cool on a wire rack while preparing filling. Reduce oven temperature to 350°F.

4 For the filling, in a small bowl combine ¾ cup sugar and ¼ cup flour; set aside. In a medium bowl beat egg yolks, 1 cup sour cream, vanilla, and lemon peel until combined. Add sugar mixture and beat until smooth.

5 Slice pears. Arrange slices slightly overlapping on crust. Pour filling over pears. Place tart pan on a baking sheet.

6 Bake 1 hour or until custard is set and lightly golden. If necessary, cover edge of tart with foil the last 5 to 10 minutes to prevent overbrowning. Cool tart to room temperature on a wire rack.

7 Spread some of the glaze over cooled tart. Pass remaining glaze. Serve tart at room temperature. Cover and refrigerate leftovers.

PER SERVING 429 **CAL**; 19 g **FAT** (11 g **SAT**); 137 mg **CHOL**; 110 mg **SODIUM**; 58 g **CARB**; 3 g **FIBER**; 5 g **PRO**

Cider-Baked Stuffed Apples with Salty Caramel Sauce

Be sure to use one of the types of apples listed below. Baking apples keep their shape better than other varieties when they're exposed to heat—and you don't want your baked apples turning to mush.

MAKES 4 servings   **PREP** 30 minutes   **SLOW COOK** 5 hours (low) or 2½ hours (high)

4	baking apples, such as Pink Lady, Honeycrisp, or Braeburn, about 2½ to 2¾ inches in diameter
⅓	cup dried cranberries, chopped
¼	cup finely chopped walnuts
¼	cup packed brown sugar
1	cup apple cider or apple juice
1	teaspoon lemon zest
2	tablespoons lemon juice
3	inches stick cinnamon
1	tablespoon butter, cut into 4 pieces
⅓	cup packed brown sugar
¼	cup whipping cream
¼	cup butter
1	tablespoon light-color corn syrup
½	teaspoon vanilla
½	teaspoon coarse sea salt
	Vanilla or cinnamon ice cream (optional)

1 Core apples; peel a strip from the top of each apple. Place apples, top sides up, in a 3½- or 4-quart slow cooker. (If necessary, trim apples to stand in the cooker.)

2 For the filling, in a small bowl combine cranberries, walnuts, and brown sugar. Spoon filling into centers of apples, patting in with a knife or narrow metal spatula. Combine apple cider, lemon zest, and juice and pour around apples. Add stick cinnamon to liquid. Top each apple with a piece of butter.

3 Cover and cook on low 5 hours or high 2½ hours.

4 Meanwhile, for the Salty Caramel Sauce,* in a small heavy saucepan bring the ⅓ cup brown sugar, whipping cream, butter, and corn syrup to boiling over medium-high heat, whisking occasionally; reduce heat to medium. Boil gently, uncovered, 2 minutes. Remove from heat. Stir in vanilla and sea salt. Cool to room temperature before serving.

5 To serve, transfer warm apples to dessert dishes. Spoon some cooking liquid over apples. Serve with Salty Caramel Sauce and, if desired, ice cream.

*For a quicker sauce, in a small saucepan stir together ½ cup caramel-flavor ice cream topping and ½ teaspoon coarse sea salt; warm through before serving.

PER SERVING 549 **CAL**; 25 g **FAT** (13 g **SAT**); 59 mg **CHOL**; 440 mg **SODIUM**; 80 g **CARB**; 7 g **FIBER**; 2 g **PRO**

Spiced Pear-Cranberry Cobbler

This pumpkin pie-spiced cobbler topped with crunchy cornmeal biscuits is a fitting finish to a fall dinner.

MAKES 8 servings **PREP** 40 minutes **BAKE** 1 hour **COOL** 30 minutes

6	medium Bosc, Anjou, and/or Asian pears, peeled, cored, and coarsely chopped (6 cups)
1	16-ounce can whole cranberry sauce
1	cup fresh cranberries or ⅓ cup dried cranberries or dried cherries
½	cup packed brown sugar
1	teaspoon pumpkin pie spice or ground cinnamon
¾	cup all-purpose flour
¼	cup cornmeal
3	tablespoons granulated sugar
1½	teaspoons baking powder
½	teaspoon pumpkin pie spice or ground cinnamon
¼	cup cold butter, cut up
1	egg, lightly beaten
½	cup canned pumpkin
2	tablespoons half-and-half, light cream, milk, or pear nectar
	Whipped cream, light cream, or vanilla ice cream

1 Preheat oven to 375°F. In a large bowl combine pears, cranberry sauce, cranberries, brown sugar, and the 1 teaspoon pumpkin pie spice. Transfer filling to a 2-quart casserole. Bake, covered, 30 minutes.

2 Meanwhile, for biscuit topping, in a medium bowl combine flour, cornmeal, the 3 tablespoons granulated sugar, baking powder, and the ½ teaspoon pumpkin pie spice. Using a pastry blender, cut butter into flour mixture until pieces are pea size. In a small bowl combine egg, pumpkin, and half-and-half. Add pumpkin mixture to flour mixture all at once, stirring just until combined.

3 Carefully remove casserole from oven. Spoon topping into eight mounds on hot pear filling. If desired, sprinkle with additional granulated sugar.

4 Bake, uncovered, 30 minutes more or until a wooden toothpick inserted near center of topping comes out clean. Cool 30 minutes. Serve warm with whipped cream.

PER SERVING 417 **CAL**; 13 g **FAT** (8 g **SAT**); 64 mg **CHOL**; 148 mg **SODIUM**; 76 g **CARB**; 6 g **FIBER**; 4 g **PRO**

Double-Chocolate Bread Pudding with Strawberry Sauce

When you want to serve a warm dessert but don't want to fuss with making it while your guests are there, this chocolatey slow-cooker bread pudding is just the thing. The strawberry sauce can be made ahead and chilled until serving time.

MAKES 8 servings   **PREP** 35 minutes   **SLOW COOK** 2½ hours (low)   **COOL** 30 minutes

	Nonstick cooking spray
3	cups whole milk
1	cup sugar
¼	cup butter
1	cup semisweet chocolate pieces
⅔	cup unsweetened cocoa powder
1	tablespoon vanilla
4	eggs, lightly beaten
6	cups dry ¾-inch Italian bread cubes*
1	16-ounce container frozen sliced strawberries in syrup, thawed
⅓	cup strawberry preserves

1 Lightly coat the crockery liner of a 3½- or 4-quart slow cooker with cooking spray.

2 In a medium saucepan heat milk, sugar, and butter over medium heat until very warm but not boiling, stirring occasionally to dissolve sugar. Remove from heat. Add chocolate pieces and cocoa powder (do not stir); let stand 5 minutes. Add vanilla. Whisk until smooth; cool slightly (about 10 minutes).

3 In an extra-large mixing bowl whisk together eggs and chocolate mixture. Gently stir in bread cubes. Transfer bread mixture to prepared cooker.

4 Cover and cook on low 2½ hours or until pudding is puffed and appears set when gently shaken. Turn off cooker. If possible, remove crockery liner from cooker and place on wire rack. Cool, uncovered, 30 minutes (pudding will fall slightly as it cools).

5 Meanwhile, for strawberry sauce, in a blender or food processor, puree strawberries along with syrup and the strawberry preserves until smooth. Cover; refrigerate until serving.

6 Spoon warm bread pudding into dessert dishes and top with strawberry sauce.

***Tip** For dried bread cubes, preheat oven to 300°F. Cut enough soft Italian bread loaf (not crusty) into ¾-inch cubes to equal 6 cups. Spread bread cubes in a 15×10×1-inch baking pan. Bake 10 to 15 minutes or until cubes are dry, stirring twice. Cool.

PER SERVING 528 **CAL**; 20 g **FAT** (11 g **SAT**); 117 mg **CHOL**; 319 mg **SODIUM**; 84 g **CARB**; 6 g **FIBER**; 11 g **PRO**

Index

Metric Information

These charts provide a guide for converting measurements from the U.S. customary system, which is used throughout this book, to the metric system.

PRODUCT DIFFERENCES

Most of the ingredients called for in the recipes in this book are available in most countries. However, some are known by different names. Here are some common American ingredients and their possible counterparts:

- Sugar (white) is granulated, fine granulated, or castor sugar.
- Confectioners' sugar is icing sugar.
- All-purpose flour is enriched, bleached or unbleached white household flour. When self-rising flour is used in place of all-purpose flour in a recipe that calls for leavening, omit the leavening agent (baking soda or baking powder) and salt.
- Light-color corn syrup is golden syrup.
- Cornstarch is cornflour.
- Baking soda is bicarbonate of soda.
- Vanilla or vanilla extract is vanilla essence.
- Green, red, or yellow sweet peppers are capsicums or bell peppers.
- Golden raisins are sultanas.

VOLUME AND WEIGHT

The United States traditionally uses cup measures for liquid and solid ingredients. The chart, top right, shows the approximate imperial and metric equivalents. If you are accustomed to weighing solid ingredients, the following approximate equivalents will be helpful.

- 1 cup butter, castor sugar, or rice = 8 ounces = ½ pound = 250 grams
- 1 cup flour = 4 ounces = ¼ pound = 125 grams
- 1 cup icing sugar = 5 ounces = 150 grams

Canadian and U.S. volume for a cup measure is 8 fluid ounces (237 ml), but the standard metric equivalent is 250 ml.

1 British imperial cup is 10 fluid ounces.

In Australia, 1 tablespoon equals 20 ml, and there are 4 teaspoons in the Australian tablespoon.

Spoon measures are used for smaller amounts of ingredients. Although the size of the tablespoon varies slightly in different countries, for practical purposes and for recipes in this book, a straight substitution is all that's necessary. Measurements made using cups or spoons should always be level unless stated otherwise.

COMMON WEIGHT RANGE REPLACEMENTS

Imperial/U.S.	Metric
½ ounce	15 g
1 ounce	25 g or 30 g
4 ounces (¼ pound)	115 g or 125 g
8 ounces (½ pound)	225 g or 250 g
16 ounces (1 pound)	450 g or 500 g
1¼ pounds	625 g
1½ pounds	750 g
2 pounds or 2¼ pounds	1,000 g or 1 Kg

OVEN TEMPERATURE EQUIVALENTS

Fahrenheit Setting	Celsius Setting*	Gas Setting
300°F	150°C	Gas Mark 2 (very low)
325°F	160°C	Gas Mark 3 (low)
350°F	180°C	Gas Mark 4 (moderate)
375°F	190°C	Gas Mark 5 (moderate)
400°F	200°C	Gas Mark 6 (hot)
425°F	220°C	Gas Mark 7 (hot)
450°F	230°C	Gas Mark 8 (very hot)
475°F	240°C	Gas Mark 9 (very hot)
500°F	260°C	Gas Mark 10 (extremely hot)
Broil	Broil	Grill

*Electric and gas ovens may be calibrated using celsius. However, for an electric oven, increase celsius setting 10 to 20 degrees when cooking above 160°C. For convection or forced air ovens (gas or electric) lower the temperature setting 25°F/10°C when cooking at all heat levels.

BAKING PAN SIZES

Imperial/U.S.	Metric
9x1½-inch round cake pan	22- or 23x4-cm (1.5 L)
9x1½-inch pie plate	22- or 23x4-cm (1 L)
8x8x2-inch square cake pan	20x5-cm (2 L)
9x9x2-inch square cake pan	22- or 23x4.5-cm (2.5 L)
11x7x1½-inch baking pan	28x17x4-cm (2 L)
2-quart rectangular baking pan	30x19x4.5-cm (3 L)
13x9x2-inch baking pan	34x22x4.5-cm (3.5 L)
15x10x1-inch jelly roll pan	40x25x2-cm
9x5x3-inch loaf pan	23x13x8-cm (2 L)
2-quart casserole	2 L

U.S./STANDARD METRIC EQUIVALENTS

⅛ teaspoon = 0.5 ml	⅓ cup = 3 fluid ounces = 75 ml
¼ teaspoon = 1 ml	½ cup = 4 fluid ounces = 125 ml
½ teaspoon = 2 ml	⅔ cup = 5 fluid ounces = 150 ml
1 teaspoon = 5 ml	¾ cup = 6 fluid ounces = 175 ml
1 tablespoon = 15 ml	1 cup = 8 fluid ounces = 250 ml
2 tablespoons = 25 ml	2 cups = 1 pint = 500 ml
¼ cup = 2 fluid ounces = 50 ml	1 quart = 1 litre